M000235250

PETER, THE POPES, AND MARY:
WHATEVER HAPPENED TO JESUS?

to Jan
For your
wonderful friendship
over many years

Paul e Wiltia

PETER, THE POPES, AND MARY:
WHATEVER HAPPENED TO JESUS?

Demolishing the
Seven Pillars of Rome

Paul I. Johnson Ph.D.

REDEMPTION
PRESS

Copyright © 2016 by Paul I. Johnson. All rights reserved.

Published by Redemption Press, PO Box 427, Enumclaw, WA 98022

Toll Free (844) 2REDEEM (273-3336)

Redemption Press is honored to present this title in partnership with the author. The views expressed or implied in this work are those of the author. Redemption Press provides our imprint seal representing design excellence, creative content, and high quality production.

No part of this publication may be reproduced, stored in a retrieval system, or transmitted in any way by any means—electronic, mechanical, photocopy, recording, or otherwise—without the prior permission of the copyright holder, except as provided by USA copyright law.

Scripture taken from the HOLY BIBLE, NEW INERNATIONAL VERSION Copyright© 1973, 1978, 1984 International Bible Society. Used by permission of Zondervan Bible Publishers.

The author takes full and complete responsibility for the entire text of this book.

ISBN: 978-1-68314-111-2

978-1-68314-113-6 ePub

978-1-68314-114-3 Mobi

Library of Congress Catalog Card Number: 2016952490

For Jared, Nathan, and their generation

TABLE OF CONTENTS

Acknowledgements, ix
Preface, xiii

Introduction, xv
    Chapter 1: Becoming a Christian, 25

Pillar One
    Chapter 2: Peter as Presented in the New Testament, 35
    Chapter 3: Was Peter the First Bishop of Rome?, 53
    Chapter 4: Peter the Rock, the Keys, and the Reality, 65

Pillar Two
    Chapter 5: The Dubious History of Popery, 85

Pillar Three
    Chapter 6: Mary, the Temporary Mother of Jesus, 109

Pillar Four
     Chapter 7: Tradition Trumps Scripture, 131
     Chapter 8: The Sacramental System Explained, 145

Pillar Five
     Chapter 9: Water Baptism, 161

Pillar Six
     Chapter 10: The Eucharist: The Magic Elixir, 175

Pillar Seven
     Chapter 11: Purgatory: The Great Ponzi Scheme, 193
     Chapter 12: One Man's Journey, 217

Bibliography, 231

Further Reading, 233

Notes, 237

ACKNOWLEDGEMENTS

NO BOOK CAN be written by committee. Neither can a book be written without a significant amount of contribution from qualified, interested, and committed help.

While doing the background reading that resulted in this book, I read approximately seventy-five authors of various persuasions and purposes. I am grateful for each of those authors who helped me to understand how and why the Catholic religious system developed as it did and why it was challenged so forcefully through the Protestant Reformation.

Not all of the authors who contributed to my understanding are listed in the bibliography. I only listed the ones who were quoted in my book and a few others I felt the reader should know about. Bibliographies in the books that are listed in my bibliography will take the reader anywhere he or she wants to go in further reading or research.

Also, I want to acknowledge the professional and technical help of my editor, Dianne Pitts. She not only did the technical editing, but she and her husband Ron provided a rent-free apartment for my wife Willie and myself while I wrote the original draft of the book. We got lots of exercise going up and down the stairs from our apartment to Dianne's working area. Ron and Dianne also entertained us with game nights, taco Tuesdays, and other treats from Ron's kitchen. Willie and I will always be grateful for their fellowship, friendship, and wonderful hospitality.

Willie was the first reader of the manuscript. From her extensive background in editing all kinds of written documents during many years as an executive secretary, she provided valuable input. Her input regarding the use of many Scripture passages was also invaluable. She is a graduate of a notable Bible school.

My son, Paul B. Johnson, was the second reader. He was a special help in suggesting different ways to phrase certain thoughts. Also, because of his advice, the manuscript has fewer pages, for which I'm sure the reader will be thankful.

As the author, I take full responsibility for any errors that might be found.

I had a few other people read the manuscript just to get their general reaction. Each one of those readers was positive about the purpose of the book and its content. They were enthusiastic about the book becoming available to pass along to some of their friends. Some suggested it be available to be used as a teaching tool for Sunday school classes and Bible studies.

There is a group of special friends who partner with Willie and me. We were missionaries for many years and during that time, we were supported by the prayers and financial support of forty people and some churches. When we retired, many of those partners stayed with us. Consequently, they have provided financial support, encouragement, and prayers in support of this book project. We are grateful.

I must end this by saying how appreciative I am for the Bible. "Thy word is true from the beginning and every one of thy righteous judgments endureth forever" (Ps. 119:160 KJV).

A hearty thank you to all,

Paul I. Johnson

PREFACE

ON OCTOBER 31, 1517, Martin Luther posted his ninety-five thesis on the door of the Wittenberg church. It was one of the most memorable and significant events in the turbulent history of Christianity. For approximately fifteen hundred years, Roman Catholicism (which one historian commented was "neither Roman nor Catholic") masqueraded as Christianity.

One of the purposes of the book you are about to read is to remind all true Christians everywhere that Catholicism is not a form of Christianity.

Another purpose is to help bring to mind the outstanding and astounding consequences of Luther's act on that day in October, 1517.

A third purpose of this book is in some measure to contribute to the celebration of the five-hundred-year anniversary on October 31, 2017, of Luther's remarkable achievement, which ushered in what is known as the Protestant Reformation.

Luther's act was remarkable in several ways. Firstly, it forced the entire Catholic world to face the fact that its religious system was in every aspect suspect when brought before the judgment of biblical truth.

Secondly, it began to bring to light that there were absolutely no historical facts that would support this religious system with its foundational dogma that Peter was the first pope. In other words, the Catholic system failed under the light of biblical truth and historical realities.

Thirdly, when Luther posted those ninety-five statements, it started a political fallout that caused several leaders and, in fact, whole countries to begin to abandon Catholicism and adopt what was, and still is, called Protestantism.

In the process of reading this book, you may find yourself questioning not just Catholicism but the Coptic religion and the Greek Orthodox religion.

Protestantism itself has much to be held accountable for. The word *Protestantism* is an umbrella term covering many so-called expressions of Christianity. Some of these expressions of Christianity are no more Christian than Catholicism. However, the purpose of this book is to expose Catholicism for what it is: the greatest heresy ever perpetrated on the face of this planet.

But what could we expect? Satan is a master deceiver. As the apostle Paul said, Satan can appear as an "angel of light."

So, this book is written in the spirit of Martin Luther and to continue the fight for truth that he began. May the world recognize what he did for true Christianity on that day of October 31, 1517. May he be widely celebrated on October 31, 2017, and may this book lend a hearty amen to that celebration.

INTRODUCTION

JESUS CAME INTO my life in March of 1958.

When I asked Jesus to come into my life, it was a desperate call. I was in the navy and had come to the understanding that if I died, there would be only one choice for me: going to hell. Heaven was out of the question. My manner of life was such that God could not possibly accept me into heaven.

So, I asked Jesus to come into my life and save me. He answered my call. I was, as the Bible explains, "born again." The first chapter of this book is devoted to explaining how to become and how to know you are a Christian.

Up to that evening in March of 1958, I had no religious background or experience. I was a religious vacuum. But as I studied the Bible and grew in the faith, I became interested in the history of Christianity and determined that someday I would give as much time as I could to reading all about the beginnings of the Christian faith—to find my roots somewhat as the seeker in Alex Haley's book, *Roots*.

The last chapter of this book will be the story of how Jesus came into my life and where I found my roots.

When I was able to retire after forty years serving with a Protestant mission organization, the opportunity came to give the time needed to read a lot of books on the history of Christianity.

I already knew quite a bit about the Protestant Reformation, but I didn't know very much about what happened in the approximately fifteen hundred years prior to that. That is, I didn't know how Christianity had developed within the historical process of the Roman Catholic religious system and its domination up to the time of the Reformation.

Perhaps you've guessed by now that I would be labeled an evangelical. I am not, however, a Baptist, Presbyterian, Methodist, Lutheran, nor am I attached to any other denomination. I graduated with a BA from a Baptist college but have kept my options open regarding churches I've attended.

What I want you to know is, as I read and studied the history of Christianity, it wasn't from a particular denominational point-of-view. However, it was from an evangelical point-of-view—that is, the firm conviction that the Bible is explicitly (without doubt or reserve) the Word of God.

Also, I had no intention of writing a book about Roman Catholicism. I was reading and studying for my own edification. But, as I became acquainted with the early history of Christianity, I became deeply troubled by the facts of that history.

I knew something of the Roman Catholic religion before I started my prolonged and serious study of Christianity. As I studied, I discovered that the bishops of Rome (later defined as popes of the Roman Catholic religion) dominated the first approximately fifteen-hundred years in the history of Christianity. This fact was a reality that demanded my attention.

Questions kept surfacing. How and why did a religion professing to be Christian but so obviously not Christian, gain such a hold on the continent of Europe and subsequently on Latin America? In fact, it now claims about one billion adherents literally encompassing the world.

Where and how did the concept of a pope take hold in the minds of millions of people and their kings? How did Peter get brought into the mix? What about Mary?

You might already know something of the suspect dogmas: Mass, indulgences, purgatory, treasury of merit, prayers to dead saints, penance, crusades, relics, celibacy, papal tradition equaling or exceeding Scripture in authority, and the sacramental system of religion.

I knew a little about some of these dogmas (teachings that one is obligated as a Catholic to believe), but what really interested me was how these teachings came into being. What were the social, religious, political, economic, and other forces that drove millions of people to buy into such heresies?

Webster's defines heresy as, "an opinion, doctrine, or practice contrary to the truth or to generally accepted beliefs or standards." Interestingly, Webster's includes in the definition this statement: "denial of a revealed truth by a baptized member of the Roman Catholic Church."

It is true that the word *heresy* came into common use during the early years of Christianity, and it was adopted by the popes to excommunicate those who denied what they were teaching. It's almost amusing, if it wasn't so tragic, that the popes labeled teachings that contradicted their teachings as heresy, while they themselves became teachers of the greatest heresies ever propagated.

Now, I've just made a serious charge. I am stating that many of the dogmas of the Roman Catholic religion are heresies. My definition of *heresy* is beliefs and teachings that directly contradict what is taught in the Bible.

The Bible is the genuine Christian's standard of all beliefs and practices. I will be unraveling some of the dogmas of the Roman Catholic religion and showing these teachings do not adhere to, and in fact are contrary to, biblical statements and principles.

In the world of deconstruction, the powerful technique called *implosion* is used to bring down massive buildings in seconds. Experts find the exact places in the structure of a building— the load bearing points, the critical structural connections—and place explosives at these points. When the explosives are detonated, the building collapses.

My intent is to place scriptural truths at some of the most critical structural connections of the Roman Catholic religious system. It is my belief that powerful biblical truths will act, metaphorically, as explosive agents, demolishing the heretical dogmas of this religious system.

The "Seven Pillars of Rome" as they are called on the title page of this book are, in my judgment: Peter, the popes, Mary, tradition, water baptism, Mass and the Eucharist, and purgatory. It is these seven dogmas that function as the fundamental religious structure supporting the entire system.

Consequently, in all but two of the chapters, as you will see in the table of contents, we will explore and demolish each of these pillars. Texts will be cited from Catholic documents and other historical resources so the reader can see the underlying rationale Catholic leaders use to support these seven pillars. The Bible will be amply cited to show clear and contradictory evidence bringing down every one of these seven pillars.

"The weapons we fight with are not the weapons of the world. On the contrary, they have divine power to demolish strongholds. We demolish arguments and every pretension that sets itself up against the knowledge of God" (2 Cor. 10:4–5).

I don't know if many Roman Catholics will read this book, but if you are a Roman Catholic, I want to make the following clear: you may be a Roman Catholic and a genuine born-again Christian. It is not for me to say who is a Christian and who is not. However, if you are a Roman Catholic, it might be well for you to examine what you believe, or claim to believe, as a member of the Roman Catholic religion. Reading this book will help you with just that. The apostle Paul wrote: "Examine yourselves to see whether you are in the faith; test yourselves. Do you not realize that Christ Jesus is in you—unless, of course, you fail the test?" (2 Cor. 13:5).

Is Christ Jesus in you? That's the test question. What is your answer? I hope it is, "Yes."

You may have been a Catholic and now have found Jesus in a real and satisfying way as Lord and Savior. But, you may also have found that you carry some of the Catholic religious baggage in your soul and spirit. You will find in this book that many Jews who came to know Jesus in a personal way had trouble shedding Judaism. Some of them never did. Peter had that problem. At least at one time in his life, Peter was seriously hindered in his growth in the Lord by his religious baggage. You will read about it in chapter 2.

So, may God use the teachings in this book to help you to let go, to not doubt that Catholicism is a deadly religious disease, and that you were fortunate by the grace of God to be free of it, or maybe not free, yet. "[But] if the Son sets you free, you will be free indeed" (John 8:36).

You may be what many call a seeker. Perhaps you've realized that you need God in your life. Perhaps you've been attending different churches or have explored different religions.

Maybe you've been interested in Roman Catholicism. If you are a seeker, be sure to read chapter 1 thoroughly.

Maybe you are like me. You've been a Christian for years and have some knowledge of Roman Catholicism but never understood how it was so different from what you believe. Maybe, too, you considered Roman Catholicism just another form of Christianity, a schism and not a heresy.

In the original meaning of *schism*, the concept of discord or disharmony was the central idea. The word did not carry the same weight as the word *heresy*. There could be schism, but the possibility of substantial agreement was there, and thus religious fellowship was still possible.

For example, in today's religious world, Roman Catholic leaders will allow their members to attend some Lutheran churches if there is no Roman Catholic Church available in that person's area.

No matter if you are a seeker, a Roman Catholic, an ex-Roman Catholic, or a reflective but uninformed Christian, by reading this book, you will be able to demolish this religious stronghold called Roman Catholicism. You will, in the process, find out how to become a Christian, and you will, through this knowledge, discover the biblical characteristics of a genuine Christian.

I trust, too, that you will discover the reasons why New Testament Christianity cannot be equated with Roman Catholicism. In terms of the New Testament, Christianity and the Roman Catholic religious system are worlds apart.

This is not a book about people. You will not find in-depth discussions about the men who claimed to be popes—the Vicars of Christ—and some of the very bad things they did. It is a book about the Catholic religious system as it conflicts with the Word of God, the Bible, and particularly how it conflicts with the New Testament. If you know the Old Testament, you will also notice how the Catholic system brought back into Christianity several Judaistic features such as priests, sacrifices, and, in general, a feeling of a law-based religion.

There will be no discussion of the wedding of secular powers with Roman Catholicism. Almost all of the historians I read pointed out that without the secular powers of Europe supporting, by their military power, the popes and their religious system, Catholicism would have never gained and held the power that it did.

And the reverse is also true that many secular leaders realized that without the support of the popes and their emissaries, they would not have been able to stay in power. It was a constant struggle, but for many years, Catholicism virtually ruled in many European and Latin American nations.

Interestingly enough, both Luther and Calvin, leaders in the Protestant Reformation, tried to wed Christianity to secular powers. Even to this day in Germany, the State financially supports Lutheran and Catholic churches. In England, the tie between church and state still exists as the Queen of England is the titular head of Anglicanism.

The Bible is the source of truth about God and his will and his plan of salvation. The Scriptures are quoted extensively in this book because, as Paul said, the Scriptures "have the divine power to demolish strongholds" (2 Cor. 10:4–5).

As you read God's Word quoted in this book, pray as the psalmist David did to, "Open my eyes that I may see wonderful things in your law" (Ps. 119:18).

Now, one last word as to why I decided to write this book. As I read, studied, and learned what you are going to read in the coming chapters, I also became aware of a disturbing fact.

I have been a Christian for fifty-eight years. I've attended a lot of different churches and been in many Sunday school classes, in some of which I was the teacher. The disturbing fact is that in those fifty-eight years, I could not remember ever hearing any Christian pastor or Sunday school teacher say anything about what you are going to read in this book.

The Catholic religious system was never presented. There were many lessons about the details of the Jehovah's Witnesses, the Mormons, and other prominent cults. But, Catholicism, for some reason, seemed to be given a pass.

I wondered if a lot of believers in Christ considered Catholicism just another form of genuine Christianity. In fact, I think that possibility is actually true. And what about all of those pastors and Sunday school teachers who never taught the truth about Catholicism.

Has there been, in fact, a kind of political correctness resident among us Christians in that we won't speak out about the Catholic heresy? Why have we given Catholicism a pass?

The reality that no one was speaking out and explaining this giant heretical religion masquerading as Christianity was what moved me to write this book. I felt and feel today that Satan has pulled one over on us. He has pulled one over on virtually the whole world for at least fifteen-hundred years.

Some Catholics who read this book might be offended and deeply hurt by what I've written. But, remember these words from the book of Proverbs: "Better is open rebuke than hidden love. Wounds from a friend can be trusted, but an enemy multiplies kisses" (Prov. 27:5–6).

I have a number of Catholic friends. I also recognize that there may be Baptists, Presbyterians, Lutherans, and others who may read this book and find that they themselves are not experiencing what has been described above as the true nature of Christianity.

If anyone is wounded by what follows in this book, please understand that I am writing as a friend.

May God bless this book in a way that it will help expose Catholicism for what it is and open the eyes of millions and lead them to the one and only Savior of the world: Jesus the Christ, the Son of the Living God.

CHAPTER 1

BECOMING A CHRISTIAN
ESTABLISHING A BASE LINE

THIS BOOK BEGINS with this chapter—Becoming a Christian—for the purpose of establishing a kind of base line, or definition, or description of how one becomes a Christian.

Some readers may refer back to this chapter should it be necessary to become clear on how a person becomes a Christian. Although I've tried to make this clear at various places in the chapters that follow, chapter 1 starts the book, so that there will always be this place to come to should an unhindered presentation of the gospel be necessary.

According to Catholicism, the Roman Catholic Church is set forth as the means of acquiring salvation. It is set forth as the means of maintaining salvation, and it is set forth as the means of gaining heaven when the believer dies. You probably also know that something called *purgatory* stands between the believer and actually arriving in heaven. But Catholicism has the believer's back on that too. There is an imagined way through and out of purgatory if the Roman Catholic believer acquires, shall we say, the right resources. More of that later.

Effectively, then, Jesus and the Holy Spirit are not essential to achieve salvation. The Roman Catholic church claims to have, and more than that, *to be* the means of salvation. This religious scheme couldn't be further from the truth that is presented to us in the Scriptures.

The Scriptures present Jesus and the Holy Spirit to us as the only means of salvation. Jesus himself said, "I am the way and the truth and the life. No one comes to the Father except through me" (John 14:6).

Is baptism into the Roman Catholic Church a substitute for Jesus—a proxy for Jesus? That is, can a person "come to the Father" by water baptism (particularly water baptism applied by a priest of the Roman Catholic Church)? What did Jesus say? The answer is obvious. Jesus said, "No one comes to the Father except through me."

Is baptism into the Roman Catholic Church a proxy for the baptism of the Holy Spirit? Regarding the Holy Spirit and baptism, here are the words of the apostle Paul: "The body is a unit, though it is made up of many parts; and though all its parts are many, they form one body. So it is with Christ. For we were all baptized by one Spirit into one body—whether Jews or Greeks, slave or free—and we were all given the one Spirit to drink" (1 Cor. 12:12–13).

The baptism of the Holy Spirit is not water baptism and has no part with water baptism, no matter who is doing the water baptism or in what manner it is done.

By the way, the NIV translation of the Bible I quote from essentially carries the same meaning as in any Roman Catholic sponsored Bible translation. I would like to say also that I firmly believe we cannot go wrong when we interpret Scripture while following this principle: When the words of Scripture make plain sense, seek no other sense.

Now, in the above passage when Jesus said, "through me," what did he mean? How would a person come through Jesus? Is there a specific way to do this?

In John's gospel, this statement is made: "He [Jesus] was in the world, and though the world was made through him, the world did not recognize him. He came to that which was his own, but his own did not receive him. Yet to all who received him, to those who believed in his name, he gave the right to become children of God—children born not of natural descent, nor of human decision or a husband's will, but born of God" (John 1:10–13).

This Scripture says, "Yet to all who received him." How does a person receive Jesus? As a simple analogy, imagine it is your birthday: a friend comes to you with a birthday present, holds a nicely wrapped gift out to you, and says, "Here, I have a gift for you."

But you don't have the gift, yet. Why not? Because you haven't taken it. Until you receive—take the gift—it is not yours. Your friend can hold it out to you all day, but until you take the gift, it isn't yours. This is what it means to receive, to believe in Jesus. When a person actually asks Jesus to come into his life—accepts Jesus as his Savior—that person has become a Christian. In the context of salvation, it is Jesus who is being received as a gift.

As it says in John 1:13, the person who receives Jesus is "born of God." In John 3:3, Jesus said to a Jewish religious leader, "I tell you the truth, no one can see the kingdom of God unless he is born again."

So, when a person receives the gift of Jesus as his Savior, he is born again.

Receiving Jesus has consequences—wonderful consequences. In John, chapter 3, Jesus went on to answer a Jewish religious leader's perplexing question. We will follow the story as it is told in John's gospel. The Jewish leader asks: "'How can a man be born when he is old?' [This Nicodemus was an older Jewish leader. Nicodemus goes on to say,] 'Surely he cannot enter a second time into his mother's womb to be born!' Jesus answered, 'I tell you the truth, no one can enter the kingdom of God unless he is born of water and the Spirit. Flesh gives birth to flesh [being born of water: human birth], but the Spirit gives birth to spirit. You should not be surprised at my saying, 'You must be born again'" (John 3:4–7).

You might have noticed as you read through this scriptural sequence that when Jesus talked about being born again, he specified it was a spiritual rebirth. He said, "the Spirit gives birth to spirit." Note the first *Spirit* is capitalized and the second *spirit* is in the lower case. The born-again process is initiated and completed by the Holy Spirit in the spirit of the individual.

The apostle Paul said it a little differently. "Therefore, if anyone is in Christ, he is a new creation; the old has gone, the new has come!" (2 Cor. 5:17).

If you are born again you are a "new creation." Do you see and understand the beauty of what God has done by his Son and through his Holy Spirit? The role of the Holy Spirit in being born again (in becoming a new creation) is a wonderful aspect of the salvation process. It's important to understand how the Holy Spirit actually makes real and effectual in the individual what Jesus accomplished when he died on the cross and when he rose again from the dead and later ascended into heaven to be at the right hand of the Father.

It's also important for you to understand that there has been no mention of any other agent (or agency) involved in the process of salvation. Specifically, there is no human agent or agency involved. That is, to be clear, the Roman Catholic religious system (the sacramental system) has no part in salvation. I will be more specific in later chapters.

Right now, I want to emphasize the role of the Holy Spirit. You might remember that when John the Baptist was engaged in his ministry of water baptism, the Jewish crowd was perplexed about who John was. Some thought he might be the Christ (the Jewish Messiah, or Savior, who had been prophesied). In the following quote, observe the shift from water baptism to the baptism of the Holy Spirit. "The people were waiting expectantly and were all wondering in their hearts if John might possibly be the Christ. John answered them all, 'I baptize you with water. But one more powerful than I will come, the thongs of whose sandals I am not worthy to untie. He will baptize you with the Holy Spirit and with fire'" (Luke 3:15–16).

Peter said in a later incident: "As I began to speak, the Holy Spirit came on them as he had come on us at the beginning. Then I remembered what the Lord had said: 'John baptized with water, but you will be baptized with the Holy Spirit'" (Acts 11:15–16).

Following is a lengthy quote from the book of Romans that will enable us to understand just what it means to be baptized with the Holy Spirit. Again, please note the operation of salvation is begun and completed by the work of Jesus and the Holy Spirit. For emphasis the word *Spirit* is italicized in the quote. Capitalization of the word *Spirit* is in the original text.

Therefore, there is now no condemnation for those who are in Christ Jesus, because through Christ Jesus the law of the

Spirit of life set me free from the law of sin and death. For what the law [by inference, any religious laws propagated by any religion or religious system] was powerless to do in that it was weakened by the sinful nature, God did by sending his own Son in the likeness of sinful man to be a sin offering. And so he condemned sin in sinful man, in order that the righteous requirements of the law might be fully met in us, who do not live according to the sinful nature but according to the *Spirit*. Those who live according to the sinful nature have their minds set on what that nature desires, but those who live in accordance with the *Spirit* have their minds set on what the *Spirit* desires. The mind of sinful man is death, but the mind controlled by the *Spirit* is life and peace; the sinful mind is hostile to God. It does not submit to God's law, nor can it do so. Those controlled by the sinful nature cannot please God. You, however, are controlled not by the sinful nature but by the *Spirit*, if the *Spirit* of God lives in you. And if anyone does not have the *Spirit* of Christ, he does not belong to Christ. But if Christ is in you, your body is dead because of sin, yet your spirit is alive because of righteousness. And if the *Spirit* of him who raised Jesus from the dead is living in you, he who raised Christ from the dead will also give life to your mortal bodies through his *Spirit*, who lives in you (Rom. 8:1–11).

It is of critical importance to understand that the process of salvation is the work of God the Father, by the Son, through the agency of the Holy Spirit. No doubt you have observed, through the Scriptures quoted, that there is absolutely no mention of any human agency or material (natural) elements like water baptism involved. In fact, the Scriptures make it pointedly clear that water baptism had no spiritual power. Remember, Peter himself said he was told by the Lord Jesus that they would be baptized by the Holy Spirit.

And as we just read in the quote from Romans, being baptized by the Holy Spirit is an absolute necessity. As the apostle Paul said, "If anyone does not have the Spirit of Christ, he does not belong to Christ."

In another one of Paul's letters, he presents the process of salvation in such a beautiful and compact way that it is impossible to misunderstand the meaning and the implications of his words. "For it is by grace you have been saved, through faith—and this not from yourselves, it is the gift of God—not by works, so that no one can boast. For we are God's workmanship, created in Christ Jesus to do good works, which God prepared in advance for us to do" (Eph. 2:8–10).

Bible scholars have always defined *grace* in these terms: "the unmerited favor and blessing of God." In this passage in Paul's letter to Ephesus, Paul establishes the fact that grace and faith are the gift of God. Gifts are not, by nature, earned. Gifts are just that, gifts. Paul further makes this clear by saying these three things:

1. This (grace and faith) is not from yourselves. There is nothing within yourself (no religious yearnings or intentions) that God acknowledges as making you somehow deserving of grace and faith.
2. The gift of grace and faith are, "not by works." None of your religious actions—good deeds—or baptism by a Roman Catholic leader are acknowledged by God as making you deserving of his gifts of grace and faith.
3. "So that no one can boast" makes it clear no one will be able to say to God, or to anyone else, "Look at me. See how good I am. See all the good works I've done. I'm good enough to enter into heaven. I was baptized by a

Roman Catholic priest." You could be baptized by the Pope, and it wouldn't do you any good.

Those three statements make it extremely clear you cannot work yourself into heaven through any of your religious good deeds, or by getting baptized by water, or giving money to the church (or to any other agency), or by any other act that makes you think you are a good person and have followed all the religious rules of your particular religion, no matter what religion you might follow.

In Luke 18:19, Jesus himself asked, "Why do you call me good?" Jesus answered his own question by saying, "No one is good—except God alone."

Paul the apostle wrote (my italics for emphasis): "As it is written: 'There is *no one* righteous, *not even one*: there is *no one* who understands, *no one* who seeks God. *All* have turned away, they have *together* become worthless; there is *no one* who does good, *not even one*'" (Rom. 3:10–12).

Are you convinced that you cannot come to God because of your own religious desires or any outward works such as water baptism? Perhaps you are a tireless worker in your church. Maybe you've even seen marvelous things happen in other people's lives through your religious works. Read in the following what Jesus said about self-righteousness. He introduces this text by saying in verse 15 of Matthew, chapter 7, "Watch out for false prophets. They come to you in sheep's clothing, but inwardly they are ferocious wolves." "Not everyone who says to me, 'Lord, Lord,' will enter the kingdom of heaven, but only he who does the will of my Father who is in heaven. Many will say to me on that day, 'Lord, Lord, did we not prophesy in your name, and in your name drive out demons and perform many miracles?' Then I will tell them plainly, 'I never knew you. Away from me, you evildoers!'" (Matt. 7:21–23).

You can see we are helpless and hopeless without these gifts from God. How do the gifts of grace and faith come to us? Remember John 1:12? "Yet to all who received him, to those who believed in his name, he gave the right to become children of God—children born not of natural descent, nor of human decision, or a husband's will, but born of God."

As Paul says in verse 10 of Ephesians, chapter 2, "For we [those who receive Jesus by grace, through faith] are God's workmanship, created in Christ Jesus to do good works, which God prepared in advance for us to do."

Observe in this passage, that the good works that come as a result this new creation, in fact are only possible if we are "created in Christ Jesus." It's important to realize that being created in Christ Jesus is a work of God: God's workmanship. The Greek word for *workmanship* is the word *poema* from which we English speakers get the word *poem* or *poetry*.

Now isn't that a wonderful way to express God's workmanship? Each believer in Jesus Christ is a creative, individual work of poetry—a work of art, if you will—and the creator of this work is God himself.

If the process of salvation is God's work, what is the role of the church—God's people—in this process? Well, it is simply to preach this good news—this gospel. And, of course, as God's people group together in local congregations or even in large networks like denominations, they have the responsibility to build up and nurture one another in the faith.

We become Christians only by receiving Jesus as our Savior. When we receive Jesus, we are born again through the agency of the Holy Spirit; we are baptized in the Spirit. We are a new creation, the workmanship of God. And being the workmanship of God, we are now able to do good works, which God always intended for us to do, but which we could not do until we were created anew in Christ Jesus.

There is no other way to become a Christian and to do the works of God.

The apostle Paul summed it all up with this one, succinct, masterful statement: "Christ in you, the hope of glory" (Col. 1:27).

The rest of this book is about demolishing the stronghold of the Roman Catholic religion. As the title of this book indicates, we will begin with Peter as he is the foundational pillar of the entire Catholic system.

Peter is so important to the supposed authority of the leaders of Catholicism, particularly of the popes, bishops, and priests, that we must begin with him.

In fact, Peter is so significant in the whole scheme of Catholicism, I felt it necessary to devote three chapters just to his history as revealed to us in the Bible. By the way, there is no other reliable source but the Bible from which to gain a true understanding of Peter's role in the founding of Christianity.

The following three chapters will bring to light, using the Bible as the historical basis for Peter's life and ministry, that Peter had no superior status among the other apostles. These chapters will also bring to light that Peter was not the "Rock" upon which Jesus would build his church, and Peter did not solely possess the "keys" of the kingdom of God.

The imploding and demolition of the Catholic religious system now begins.

CHAPTER 2

PETER AS PRESENTED IN THE NEW TESTAMENT

PETER IS MENTIONED approximately 175 times in the New Testament, plus he is generally credited with writing 1 and 2 Peter. The four Gospels give him almost equal time, and the book of Acts has many significant references to him. His encounters with the apostle Paul are an important aspect of Paul's letter to the Galatians.

In short, Peter as a disciple in the days of Jesus' ministry on this earth is so well established it cannot be questioned. Peter was the first male disciple to look into the empty tomb. Peter was not only a disciple, he was one of the original twelve apostles.

A disciple and apostle, yes, but was Peter a pope? This question will be the focus of this chapter.

Catholics declare that he was the first pope. When they write about the men who followed Peter as popes, Catholics say that these subsequent popes "sit on Peter's throne." This means subsequent popes (some good, some bad, and some ugly—we'll look at this in a later chapter) all inherited Peter's right to absolute authority over the kingdom of God on earth.

When I first read in some Catholic writings that Peter had a throne, it seemed so incongruous with what I knew of Peter from reading the New Testament, it set my teeth on edge. Where is the evidence Peter set himself up as some kind of exalted religious authority?

Further, I also read that Peter's original throne is in Rome. It is asserted that Peter's remains are buried in Rome. What is the evidence that Peter was ever in Rome?

The assertions go even deeper as Peter (only and exclusively) is declared to be the rock upon which Jesus would build his church. It is also asserted that Jesus gave to Peter the keys of the kingdom of heaven, meaning Peter could determine who was allowed into heaven and who was not allowed in. And, of course, subsequent popes who sat on Peter's throne inherited Peter's status and authority: possessing the keys.

Establishing Peter's authority as the first pope is so important to the Roman Catholic religious structure that, if disproved, the whole system collapses just as if it were an imploding building. In his book, *Keepers of the Keys*, Nicolas Cheetham makes a telling statement: "But as regards the date and circumstances of St Peter's arrival in Rome our information is a blank. . . . The lack of any concrete evidence of the later stage of his life and of his relationship with Paul at the time of the latter's residence at Rome is very puzzling. Many scholars . . . have questioned whether he was in Rome at all. . . . If it was just a legend . . . the origin and meaning of the papacy would of course be invalidated."[1]

I intend to prove to you that Peter as the first pope is a hoax and a myth, and that the "origin and meaning of the papacy [is] invalidated."

In this chapter, the focus will be on Peter as he is presented to us in the Gospels, the book of Acts, and other related passages in the New Testament. In the following, there is no intention on my part to discredit, demean, or denounce Peter. The point will be to demonstrate through Peter's life, as presented to us in the New Testament, that Peter was not considered a special apostle; therefore, there was no reason to consider him as the first Vicar of Christ (Jesus' representative to all other people on this earth).

First of all, the meaning of the term *pope* is *papa* or *father*. It is apparent from reading Catholic literature and interacting with Catholics that male leadership figures are addressed as father. Technically, they are all, then, being addressed as pope, because that is the meaning of the word: father/pope/papa.

But, as we know, the term *pope* is reserved for the reigning pontiff.

What did Jesus say about calling anyone, "Father?"

> Then Jesus said to the crowds and to his disciples: "The teachers of the law and the Pharisees sit in Moses' seat. . . . Everything they do is done for men to see. They make their phylacteries wide and tassels on their garments long; they love the place of honor at banquets and the most important seats in the synagogues; they love to be greeted in the marketplaces and to have men call them 'Rabbi.' But you are not to be called 'Rabbi' for you have only one Master and you are all brothers. And do not call anyone on earth 'father,' for you have one Father, and he is in heaven. Nor are you to be called 'teacher,' for you have one Teacher, the Christ" (Matt. 23:1–10).

Obviously, Jesus means we should not designate certain people with terms such as rabbi, father, or teacher. "You are all brothers" is Jesus' interpretation and application of what he taught in this passage thus leveling the playing field. In the Roman Catholic system, the use of the term *pope* or *father* implies the person so addressed is in some way better or closer to God, more holy, and possessing spiritual authority over lesser Catholics.

Isn't it interesting that the entire Roman Catholic system is based upon doing something that Jesus cautioned us not to do: calling someone "Father."

Can you imagine, if you have any understanding of the nature of Jesus, that he would approve of calling anyone pope or father in a Christian setting where all are brothers and sisters by virtue of their relationship to him? Can you imagine Peter adopting the title of Pope? Can you imagine Peter setting himself upon a throne above every other apostle? Can you imagine the other apostles allowing Peter to do this? If you can imagine such things, you haven't read the New Testament.

Let's take a look at Peter both before the day of Pentecost when the Holy Spirit came upon those who believed in Christ and then what happened in Peter's life and experience after that wonderful, spiritually powerful day.

Most people know Peter was an impetuous personality. He has been singled out in the Gospels as the disciple of Jesus who was consistently saying and doing things that got him into trouble with Jesus. We might in today's language say that he was always putting his foot in his mouth.

Remember when Jesus walked across the lake on the water and Peter called out to Jesus to help him walk on the water, too? Peter got a few steps out on the water, became afraid, and began to sink. Jesus rescued Peter and said to him, "You of little faith . . . why did you doubt?" (Matt. 14:31).

In another incident, Jesus asked Peter who people are saying that, he, Jesus is. And, then, Jesus asked Peter:

"Who do you say that I am?" Simon Peter answered; "You are the Christ, the Son of the living God." Jesus replied. "Blessed are you, Simon son of Jonah, for this was not revealed to you by man, but by my Father in heaven. And I tell you that you are Peter, and on this rock I will build my church, and the gates of Hades will not overcome it. I will give you the keys of the kingdom of heaven; whatever you bind on earth will be bound in heaven, and whatever you loose on earth will loosed in heaven" (Matt. 16:15–19).

You would think after such a confession on Peter's part and after Jesus said such wonderful things about Peter, that Peter could do no wrong. He is the rock upon which Jesus is going to build the church, and he is being given the keys to the kingdom of heaven, or so it seems.

However, right after that exchange, Jesus began to explain to the disciples that he must go to Jerusalem, and he will be killed by the priests and teachers of the law, and he will rise from the dead on the third day. Peter follows up Jesus' statements with this: "Peter took him aside and began to rebuke him, 'Never, Lord!' he said. 'This shall never happen to you!' Jesus turned and said to Peter. 'Get behind me, Satan! You are a stumbling block to me; you do not have in mind the things of God, but the things of men'" (Matt. 16:22–23).

It is obvious Peter had no absolute corner on the truth, nor as we saw in the incident of walking on the water, Peter had no absolute corner on a strong faith either. Jesus actually called Peter, Satan. That speaks loud and clear that Peter was totally out of touch with who Jesus was and what Jesus was about at that moment. Jesus, in effect, said to Peter, "You are acting like my worst enemy!"

A third incident in Peter's life, his betrayal of Jesus on the night preceding Jesus' crucifixion, was predicted by Jesus. It happened just as Jesus said it would: "Now Peter was sitting out in the courtyard, and a servant girl came to him. 'You also were with Jesus of Galilee,' she said. But he denied it before them all. 'I don't know what you're talking about,' he said" (Matt. 26:69–70).

You probably know this story well, so I won't quote the whole passage, but at the end, it is said of Peter, after three denials, "And he went outside and wept bitterly" (Matt. 26:75).

So, the question comes up, did Peter change in any significant way after the resurrection and the coming of the Holy Spirit as recorded in the first chapter of the book of Acts?

Yes, he did. We learn from Luke that on the day of Pentecost, in Acts 2:14–26, Peter was then publically proclaiming to a large audience in Jerusalem the life and resurrection of Jesus and the coming of the Holy Spirit. The apostle Paul also tells us:

> For what I received I passed on to you as of first importance: that Christ died for our sins according to the Scriptures, and that he was buried, that he was raised on the third day according to the Scriptures, and that he appeared to Peter, and then to the Twelve. After that, he appeared to more than five hundred of the brothers at the same time, most of whom are still living, though some have fallen asleep [died]. Then he appeared to James, then to all the apostles, and last of all he appeared to me also, as to one abnormally born (1 Cor. 15:3–8).

As Paul said, "he appeared to Peter." We have no record of what occurred at this meeting between the resurrected Jesus and the disciple who betrayed him. But the result in Peter's life is evidence something took place that caused Peter to continue as an outspoken, public leader among the followers of Jesus.

It's important for our understanding to realize that, at this time, most of the followers of Jesus were Jews. Peter's primary ministry would be to the Jews.

It is through the book of Acts, Galatians, 1 Corinthians and the two books, 1 and 2 Peter that we can best judge whether Peter became the first pope—the top apostle. Was Peter the leader of the whole body of believers who existed at this time and who became scattered all around that part of the world? Did Peter ever sit on his papal throne in Rome?

The following incidents in Peter's life and ministry will reveal Peter's role in the early church, what he thought about himself, and specifically, his relationship to the apostle Paul. It will also reveal how his relationship with Paul came to determine Peter's role in the spread of the gospel to the Gentile world.

The Bible is very clear that Peter's primary ministry was to the Jews and Paul's primary ministry was to the Gentiles. Paul said in Galatians: "As for those who seemed to be important—whatever they were makes no difference to me; God does not judge by external appearance—those men added nothing to my message. On the contrary, they saw that I had been entrusted with the task of preaching the gospel to the Gentiles, just as Peter had been to the Jews. For God who was at work in the ministry of Peter as an apostle to the Jews, was also at work in my ministry as apostle to the Gentiles" (Gal. 2:6–8).

The above passage is important for our understanding of Peter's position among the other apostles and how he and the apostles were viewed by Paul. Paul said, "As for those who seemed to be important—whatever they were makes no difference to me; God does not judge by external appearance—those men added nothing to my message."

There was an outward appearance of importance. Peter and some of the other apostles had many experiences while in direct contact with Jesus before and after Jesus' resurrection. Peter had introduced the Holy Spirit to a large crowd of Jews in Jerusalem on the day of Pentecost. Peter was, on some other important occasions, the spokesman for other apostles at public gatherings. Peter "seemed to be important."

But note, not Peter nor any of the other apostles added anything to Paul's message. Peter, specifically, had no insight into or authority over what God had given Paul to preach and teach as will become clear in the next few paragraphs.

It also becomes apparent from reading further into the book of Galatians that Paul and Peter had a serious misunderstanding of what the message was. We will look into this controversy as Paul reports it in Galatians. But first, a bit of history.

As things progressed in the life of the New Testament church, a serious problem kept cropping up. At first, most of the new believers in Christ were Jews. The apostles were all Jews. But Jesus had said to his disciples in Matthew 28:19, "Therefore go and make disciples of all nations, baptizing them in the name of the Father and of the Son and of the Holy Spirit."

The Jewish apostles and other Jewish believers were reluctant, even refused, to preach the gospel to Gentiles (people who were not Jews). To the Jew, Gentiles were unclean. Gentiles weren't circumcised and did not live by the law of Moses. Jews weren't even allowed to eat with a Gentile. Eating with a Gentile would mean that the Jew considered the Gentile a brother.

They simply could not do this under their current Old Testament belief system.

Even for Peter, this was a serious problem. The Lord, of course, knew that this was a problem in Peter's life and conscience. The Lord was, in fact, sending a Gentile named Cornelius to Peter for the very purpose of hearing the gospel from Peter. The Lord prepared Peter for this encounter by giving him a vision. (This story is recorded in Acts, chapter 10.) In the vision, Peter saw a kind of sheet coming down from heaven, and in the sheet were numerous kinds of animals. These animals were all unclean to the Jew. That is, Jews could not eat these animals.

But the Lord told Peter to eat. Peter refused the Lord's command and cited his (Peter's) life-long commitment to never eat anything impure or unclean. Then, the Lord said to Peter (three times), "Do not call anything impure that God has made clean" (Acts 10:15).

In the meantime, the Lord had spoken to Cornelius that a certain man named Peter had a message from God for him. So, the next day, after Peter's vision of the unclean animals that were really clean, messengers from Cornelius came and asked Peter to come to Cornelius' house to share God's message. Because of the vision, Peter was now ready to share the gospel with Gentiles.

The story that Peter had preached to Gentiles and that those Gentiles had received Jesus and the Holy Spirit and were baptized, got back to the apostles and elders in Jerusalem. In fact, among this leadership group, there were some who didn't think it was right that Peter should be going to Gentiles. These were the Jews who held that, even though you might believe in Jesus, you still had to be circumcised and follow the Jewish (Moses') laws of behavior, and you certainly couldn't eat with a

Gentile. This was Peter's belief before the sheet that came down from heaven had appeared to him in a vision.

Peter went to the apostles and elders in Jerusalem and told them the whole story. They seemed glad to hear how God was working among the Gentiles. Peter's concluding remark at the end of the meeting was: "So if God gave them the same gift as he gave us [the gift of the Holy Spirit], who believed in the Lord Jesus Christ, who was I to think that I could oppose God. [The apostles and elders then concluded] So then, God has granted even the Gentiles repentance unto life" (Acts 11:17–18).

However, this was not to be the end of the matter: enter the apostle Paul and Barnabas. Paul and Barnabas had just returned to Antioch from their first venture into preaching the gospel in a number of cities beyond Antioch. The church at Antioch had sent them out under the direction of the Holy Spirit.

Paul felt they needed to report to the apostles and elders in Jerusalem what God had been doing among the Jews and Gentiles in the cities where they had preached. There had been intense opposition, even to the point of attempts on their lives. That opposition was instigated by Jews.

As a matter of note, there seemed to be three Jewish groups opposing the gospel message: Jews who held tightly to the Jewish religion and denied Jesus was the Christ, Grecian Jews who held onto their Jewish heritage but tried to adopt and adapt the thoughts of Greek philosophers into Judaism, and Jews who believed that Jesus was their Messiah but also believed that even if you received Jesus that you had to be circumcised and follow Jewish rules coming down through Moses. Even these believers caused constant trouble within the Christian gatherings because they wouldn't eat with Gentile Christians. There was a strong racial/religious bias present. Later we will see this surface in Peter's life when he visited Paul in Antioch.

But back to the story as it is unfolded in Jerusalem before the council of apostles and elders. When Paul and Barnabas appeared in Jerusalem to report, there was strong opposition from the Jewish believers who would not eat with Gentile believers because the Gentiles hadn't been circumcised and didn't follow the law of Moses. In other words, these Jewish believers would not fellowship with Gentile believers. This caused confusion and hard feelings between the two groups of believers.

At the meeting, in the midst of the opposition to Paul and Barnabas, Peter stood up and told again his personal experience of the sheet coming down from heaven, his new understanding that the gospel was to go to the Gentiles, and the results of preaching the gospel to Cornelius and his family.

As a result, James (the brother of Jesus) stood up and said:

> Brothers, listen to me, Simon has described to us how God at first showed his concern by taking from the Gentiles a people for himself. The words of the prophets are in agreement with this. . . . It is my judgment, therefore, that we not make it difficult for the Gentiles who are turning to God. Instead we should write to them" (Acts 15:13–20).

> Then the apostles and elders, with the whole church, decided to choose some of their own men and send them to Antioch with Paul and Barnabas. . . . With them they sent a letter: [with this heading] The apostles and elders, your brothers, To the Gentile believers in Antioch, Syria and Cilicia (Acts 15:22–23).

Please note in the above (much of which I have not quoted) these things:

1. Peter wasn't a leader in this group of apostles and elders; at least he wasn't singled out as a leader.
2. The decision was made by "the apostles and elders, with the whole church."
3. James was the active leader, not Peter. It was James who said, "It is my judgment."
4. Even after James said, "It is my judgment," he repeatedly made it clear the decision to write the letter to the church at Antioch and the decision as to what to say in that letter was a joint decision. James used the third person, *we*, four times to make sure the decision is perceived as a joint decision.
5. Most important, for the purposes of this chapter in this book, there is not the slightest hint of Peter being perceived as a universal leader of the whole church. (He wasn't even the leader in this group of apostles and elders.) There wasn't the slightest notion of any one of the apostles, much less Peter, being a pope (the Father and infallible leader of all Christians). To imagine from this decision-making process, or any other like situation in the book of Acts, that any one apostle is destined to sit on a throne in Rome and command the whole world of Christians is completely ridiculous. It makes one amazed that this misrepresentation is exactly what the Roman Catholics have been using to deceive many Christians and the general public for hundreds of years.

As was said above, this problem (the conflict between Jewish and Gentile Christians) isn't over yet, especially in Peter's life. It turns out that later Peter decided to visit Paul in Antioch, and while Peter was there, the following situation occurred. Paul reports: "When Peter came to Antioch, I opposed him to his face, because he was clearly in the wrong. Before certain men came from James, he used to eat with the Gentiles. But when they arrived, he began to draw back and separate himself from the Gentiles because he was afraid of those who belonged to the circumcision group. The other Jews joined him in his hypocrisy, so that by their hypocrisy even Barnabas was led astray" (Gal. 2:11–13).

It's a serious charge to be called a hypocrite. Yet, that is exactly what Paul called Peter. He also charged Peter with (implied) cowardice and with leading others into hypocrisy, even Barnabas. Peter's actions are particularly difficult to understand when we think back on two incidents that make it appear that Peter had left behind the spiritual baggage of Judaism (you have to be circumcised and follow the law of Moses).

Why did Paul call Peter a hypocrite? It was because of what Peter said in that prior meeting in Jerusalem. Peter had defended Paul and Barnabas and had done so by relating, once again to the apostles and elders, his own experience with Cornelius.

So, what has happened? We find Peter refusing to eat with Gentiles in Antioch but only when certain Jews appeared. Paul calls Peter a hypocrite. Is this any way to speak to a future pope? How could Peter have known the Gentiles (by his own special experience from God) were accepted by God and yet refuse to eat with them "for fear of the Jews"?

We should note also that it was fear of the Jews who "came from James" that caused Peter's retraction and hypocrisy. This implies that Peter considered James superior to himself, otherwise why would he be afraid of these men who were representing the circumcision group and who had come from James? Paul made a special note of James being behind this group's presence.

47

Remember, it was because of fear that Peter denied Christ Jesus three times during the night of Jesus' betrayal, leading up to the crucifixion.

Like a lot of us who believe, Peter had to deal with fear when it came to standing up for Jesus. And there were two times, once before Pentecost and once after, Peter failed this test.

Peter said something about himself in one of his own writings that reveals he was not an infallible interpreter of the Bible, as is claimed by the popes. "Bear in mind that our Lord's patience means salvation, just as our dear brother Paul also wrote you with the wisdom that God gave him. He writes the same way in all his letters, speaking in them of these matters. His letters contain some things that are hard to understand, which ignorant and unstable people distort, as they do the other Scriptures, to their own destruction" (2 Peter 3:15–16).

Peter admits that Paul's letters speak of things that are hard to understand. By this admission, Peter reveals his own lack of understanding of the Scriptures (at least in reference to Paul's letters). He admits Paul wrote things that he, Peter (among others), had a hard time understanding.

It's important to note from reading the book of Acts that Peter is dropped out of the picture just over halfway through the book. His last appearance is (ironically, in defense of Paul and Barnabas and their preaching to the Gentiles) in chapter 15. There are twenty-seven chapters in the book of Acts. If you are mathematically inclined, you will quickly compute that Peter is mentioned in only the first 65 percent of Acts.

Interestingly, we have in the book of Acts the foundation and life of the early days of the young church, and Peter is dropped out of that picture before we get just beyond the halfway point. We must conclude that the Holy Spirit who inspired the book written by Luke did not think Peter's ministry to the Jews was as important as Paul's ministry to the greater world: the Gentiles.

Except for Paul's negative reference to Peter in Galatians and three comments in 1 Corinthians, Paul never mentions Peter again. In fact, two of Paul's comments involving Peter in this letter are quite interesting. (Cephas in the following is another name for Peter.)

> My brothers, some from Chloe's household have informed me that there are quarrels among you. What I mean is this: One of you says, "I follow Paul"; another, "I follow Apollos"; another "I follow Cephas"; still another, "I follow Christ." Is Christ divided? Was Paul crucified for you? Were you baptized into the name of Paul? I am thankful that I did not baptize any of you except Crispus and Gaius, so no one can say that you were baptized into my name (1 Cor. 1:11–15).

> So then, no more boasting about men! All things are yours, whether Paul or Apollos or Cephas or the world or life or death or the present or the future—all are yours, and you are of Christ, and Christ is of God (1 Cor. 3:21–23).

Can we not see how clearly Paul is leveling the playing field among these three preachers of the gospel? Cephas (Peter) is on the same level with Paul and Apollos. "So then, no more boasting about men!" is Paul's word to us on this issue; the issue of establishing some kind of hierarchy among the apostles.

By the way, in this teaching by Paul, Apollos is put on the same level with Paul and Peter, and Apollos isn't even one of the twelve apostles. And, note too, this isn't Paul's final word. In his final word, he says, "All are yours, and you are of Christ, and Christ is of God," and makes it very clear by that last statement—all are yours—that we believers do not need to rely upon, nor exalt any one of God's messengers above any other of God's messengers. Believers do not belong to these preachers. Their spiritual gifts, ministries, and writings belong to us.

In the above, the main point is that Peter was not considered to be of any more importance than any of the other of God's gifted teachers and preachers.

Other than the above references, Peter drops out of sight in the New Testament. Of course, we have Peter's own writings known as 1 and 2 Peter. But Peter is never mentioned (other than in the Gospels and texts already referenced) by any of the other writers of New Testament documents including John's three letters, plus the book of Revelation, and the books of James, Jude, and Hebrews.

It's especially significant that John never mentions Peter in any of his letters or in the book of Revelation. It was John who accompanied Peter on some of the most exciting and memorable experiences in the early days as recorded in the book of Acts. They were imprisoned together. They did signs and wonders together as a two-man team.

Doesn't it seem strange that if Peter was an exalted apostle who was to reign over the whole Christian world, wouldn't you expect him to be the prominent and dominant person brought to your attention throughout the book of Acts and also in the other books of the New Testament; if by no one else, surely by John who was it seems Peter's best friend?

In fact, the opposite occurs. Peter is withdrawn from the action; it seems almost deliberately, which if that is so, it was the Holy Spirit (God himself) who directed Peter's disappearance from the life of the young church as they interacted with and spread out to the Gentile world.

There seems to be an echo here—an echo of John the Baptist's testimony about himself and Jesus. In John 3:30, the Baptist said, "He must become greater; I must become less."

Why have men and women made such an attempt to exalt Peter and his supposed successors as the world leaders of Christianity? This exaltation of Peter promoted by a worldwide religion called Roman Catholicism may be the greatest heresy the world has ever known.

In the next chapter, we will probe deeper into this great heresy as we explore various aspects of Peter's history. We will start with the greatest hoax ever perpetrated in the name of Peter.

CHAPTER 3

WAS PETER THE FIRST BISHOP OF ROME?

IN THE PREVIOUS chapter, Peter was seen as he really was within the framework of the Gospels and how he appeared in the book of Acts and other selected Scriptures. And we saw that Peter did not have apostolic primacy: being the first and foremost among the apostles, including his position as the top apostle with worldwide authority and as Jesus' personal representative—the Vicar of Christ.

Of course, the Roman Catholic religion promotes Peter with apostolic primacy. Then, it creatively projects that primacy upon the chain of so-called popes beginning with the first bishop of Rome and extending throughout the entire chain of over 295 popes; Francis being the current pope.

But as was shown in the previous chapter, Peter was never accorded any primacy by the other apostles and leaders of the church as developed in the book of Acts, nor was he as we saw him in action in other Scriptures. In fact, other than Peter's fulfillment of his special role in the young church, he was actually removed from the action.

It was noted that after chapter 15 of Acts, Peter had no place in the further foundation and growth of the Gentile church. Yes, he is mentioned by Paul in two of Paul's letters (1 Corinthians and Galatians). However, in Paul's comments about Peter, two instances simply bear out the reality Peter was not considered special by Paul, and in one of those encounters, Paul calls Peter a hypocrite.

As a reminder, Paul called Peter a hypocrite because of Peter's fear of the Jews from Jerusalem. Because of this fear, Peter would not eat with the Gentile believers in Antioch when Jews came up from Jerusalem to visit them. Apparently, Peter brought some serious religious baggage into his new relationship with Jesus (his post-resurrection relationship).

Remember the time when the sheet filled with all kinds of unclean animals was presented to him in a vision, and he told the Lord he had never eaten anything unclean?

Was Peter not only a hypocrite, but also convinced of his own righteousness under Moses' law; that is, leaning toward self-righteousness? At any rate, we find Peter removed from an active role, at least removed from the written record left to us by the hand of Luke. He is withdrawn from the ongoing foundation and growth of the church as it spread out into the Gentile world.

We can postulate that Peter was not qualified because of his possible self-righteousness and self-evident hypocrisy to further participate in that missionary enterprise: going into all the world. Therefore, as Paul said in Galatians 2:8, "For God, who was at work in the ministry of Peter as an apostle to the Jews, was also at work in my ministry as an apostle to the Gentiles." Peter's role was confined to a ministry to the Jews.

We will look into that as it impacts the reasons I conclude Peter was never in Rome. But, first, some background on that issue.

In the previous chapter, the historian Cheetham was quoted "But as regards the date and circumstances of St Peter's arrival in Rome our information is a blank. . . . Many scholars . . . have questioned whether he was in Rome at all. . . . If it was just a legend . . . the origin and meaning of the papacy would of course be invalidated." [1]

For the following reasons, I am among those who don't believe Peter was ever in Rome and consequently could not have been the first bishop of Rome and could not have been the foundation of popery. And, if these reasons add up to irrefutable evidence, "the origin and meaning of the papacy [will be] invalidated." You be the judge.

The points in one through ten that follow are not in any order of importance, and it must be admitted that some of these points are based upon circumstance not proven, historical fact. Also, number ten below required a lengthier explanation than the first nine points. The two ideas—Peter was not ever in Rome and that there was no bishop in Rome during the historical period in view—are counterpoints to some of the ten points. That is, if there was no bishop in Rome, and Peter was the touted first bishop in Rome, and Peter cannot ever be placed in Rome, well, you just can't have one without the other. And, the facts are, neither Peter as bishop of Rome or a pope existed at the time Paul wrote the book of Romans.

1. In Paul's letter to the Romans, there is no mention of Peter. At the end of the letter (Rom. 16:1–16), he names at least twenty-six individuals, plus a couple of

households, to whom he sends greetings. Paul sends no greeting to Peter.

2. You may say, "Well, maybe Peter wasn't there at the time, so why would he name Peter?" Ok, but isn't it reasonable, if not logical, that if Peter was the first bishop of Rome, Paul would have been sure to include the bishop in his greetings? And, if it wasn't Peter, who was it? The fact is, there was no bishop in Rome at the time, which is just another way of affirming Peter wasn't there: no bishop, no Peter.

3. The church at Rome, at the time Paul wrote, was made up of mostly Gentiles. We already know that Peter was, of the original apostles, the one specifically sent to the Jews. Why would Peter go to Rome if it was mostly Gentiles? Remember, beginning with chapter 15 of the book of Acts, Peter disappears as the gospel begins to spread to the Gentiles. Peter, in fact disappears from the book of Acts.

4. One of Paul's operating principles was stated in Romans 15:20, "It has always been my ambition to preach the gospel where Christ was not known, so that I would not be building on someone else's foundation." It is inconceivable that if Peter were the bishop of Rome, Paul would have written his letter to the Romans, or, at the least, it would have contained some apology to the bishop for encroaching upon that bishop's territory. There was no bishop in Rome at the time of Paul's letter, certainly not Peter.

5. As Cheetham said, "Peter's arrival in Rome . . . is a blank."[2] I've read several books dealing with this question, and not one of them has offered evidence of Peter ever having been in Rome. Do you think Cheetham

would not have brought forth the evidence if such existed? Instead, he admitted there is no evidence and many historians agree there is no evidence.

6. If an apostle such as Peter (the rock and the holder of the keys) were in Rome, or ever had been there, do you think Paul would have needed to write such a foundational document as the book of Romans? Certainly Peter would already have been teaching them.

7. The book of Acts ends with Paul being imprisoned in Rome and eventually losing his life there. Peter is never mentioned by Luke as being present in Rome at the time of Paul's arrival in Rome or during his imprisonment.

8. When Paul arrives in Rome, Luke tells us in Acts 28:17, "Three days later [after he had arrived] he called together the leaders of the Jews." If Peter were there, or had been there, why would it be necessary for Paul to preach to the Jewish leaders? Peter was the one with the mission to the Jews. But, Paul does preach to these Jews, and they for the most part refuse his message. Paul tells them, because of their rejection, he will now go to the Gentiles. Again, it is clear Peter wasn't there and wasn't the bishop of Rome.

9. A church leader named Clement who was a bishop of Rome wrote a letter about AD 96. In the letter Clement mentions Peter but makes no reference to Peter ever having been in Rome.[3]

10. When Peter wrote the epistle known as 1 Peter, at the end of this letter, he said, "She who is in Babylon, chosen together with you, sends you her greetings, and so does my son Mark" (1 Peter 5:13). It is stated by some Catholic apologists that the word *Babylon* is a reference

to Rome. However, according to the NIV Bible introductory notes to 1 Peter, "there is no evidence that the term Babylon was used figuratively to refer to Rome until Revelation was written (c. A.D. 95)," which was after Peter's life had ended.

But, Catholic apologists say it is proof that Peter was in Rome when he wrote First Peter. And, therefore, it is proof he could have been the first bishop of Rome. Certainly we can see through this fabrication.

One thing that helps us become clear on this is to realize that Peter was very likely in the real Babylon, or that vicinity, when he wrote his letter. Thousands of Jews lived in the region of Babylon as a result of the various diasporas. The Assyrians and the Babylonians deported thousands of Jews to the region of which Babylon was a kind of center. Peter's ministry was to the Jews. The Jews were massed in the area of Babylon. It makes plain sense that Peter's reference to Babylon was natural and identified his location when he wrote this letter.

Throwing all credulity aside, even if Babylon was meant to be Rome in Peter's letter, it doesn't translate into Peter thus being the bishop of Rome. Being in Rome doesn't make a person bishop of Rome. If this is all the Catholic apologists have to offer as proof of Peter's being the first pope, well, their argument is woefully without substance and merit. It is a hoax.

Now, it may seem to you that I have gone to a lot of trouble, and maybe a little redundancy, to prove that Peter was never in Rome, and, specifically, never the bishop of Rome (the first pope). But, let's remember what is at stake. In the judgment, once again, of Cheetham, "But as regards the date and circumstances of St Peter's arrival in Rome, our information is blank."

And, "If it is just a legend . . . the origin and meaning of the papacy would of course be invalidated."

The historical record is a blank. It is just a legend and poorly conceived at that. The whole Roman Catholic religious system is, therefore, invalidated.

Those are not my words. Those are the words of a noted historian. If the historical record is a blank, how have Catholic writers justified declaring Peter to have been in Rome and having been the first bishop (therefore, pope) of Rome?

We can look to Cheetham, himself, for the answer as this historian has to find some way to fill in the blank. From reading Cheetham's book, it seemed obvious he was either a Roman Catholic or certainly a friend of that religion. It will amaze you, I'm sure, as it did me the way Cheetham covers the desperate need for fact and the way he substitutes fact with revisionist history (alteration of history).

Cheetham revised history this way: "What surely matters is the strength of tradition, handed down from the early days of Christianity in Rome and fortified rather than weakened by modern scholarship and archaeology, that both the Apostles lived and were martyred in the city. It is irrelevant that the tradition later became encrusted with legend. In its original and simple form, it leaves no room for doubt. . . ." [4]

"What surely matters is the strength of tradition," so said Cheetham. As an historian, it startles me that Cheetham would appeal to tradition rather than historical fact to support the one truth (the central column of the structure of Roman Catholicism) that must stand if we are to believe Peter was the first pope. It must stand, too, if we are to believe in the whole Roman Catholic religious system. Cheetham himself said, "the origin and meaning of the papacy would of course be invalidated." If the origin and meaning is invalidated, the whole system crumbles: implodes.

In the quote above, Cheetham also said the whole system is "fortified rather than weakened by modern scholarship and archaeology." He offers no proof of such scholarship and archaeology. As far as I can determine, it boils down to a few bones that were dug up under St. Peter's Basilica that were claimed to be Peter's. If the whole system rests on Peter having been the bishop of Rome (first pope), surely there is more proof than a pile of bones. And, surely, an historian of Cheetham's caliber would demand that proof.

Cheetham also said that it is "irrelevant that the tradition later became encrusted with legend." Irrelevant? How could it be irrelevant that the original tradition became encrusted with legend? The original story was based upon tradition (because, as Cheetham admitted, the historical record is blank). And, then he implied that it was later that the original story became encrusted with legend. What kind of double talk is this? It's the kind of double talk that is characteristic of the whole account.

When the word *tradition* is used to support truth, rather than historical fact, we must ask why we should believe such a tradition. The answer comes back: "Believe it because we say it is so." That is the only authority upon which Roman Catholic tradition rests: the word of some person, or persons with no other objective fact to support that word. We are asked to believe that Peter was in Rome and the bishop of Rome simply because they said it is so; it's their tradition.

Diarmaid MacCulloch, in his book, *Christianity, the First Three Thousand Years*, made this observation: "It is unclear whether Peter had actually played the role of bishop in the Church in Rome, even if he did indeed die in the city, and the names traditionally provided for his successor bishops up to the end of the first century are no more than names. They are probably the result of later second-century back-projection to create history for the episcopal succession in the era when episcopal succession had become significant."[5]

When MacCulloch said, "the names traditionally provided," he was pointing out that there is no historical record to support the claim that Peter actually was a bishop of Rome and that the men who supposedly succeeded him have no historical credence as bishops of Rome, either.

MacCulloch put his finger right on the crux of the matter when he said it was "probably . . . back-projection to create history." It wasn't probably back-projection to create history, it *was* back-projection. When there is a blank space in the historical record and it needs to be creatively filled, one resorts to back-projection.

What does MacCulloch mean by *back-projection*? As the history of Roman Catholicism developed, there came a time when the bishops of Rome began to be called popes. Now this didn't happen immediately, but MacCulloch doesn't say when it happened. When did it happen? According to Cheetham, "the successors of St. Peter were Linus and Cletus (or Anencletus), shadowy figures who are each allotted twelve years of office."[6]

Cheetham also added, "While it may be convenient to describe them as 'Popes,' it must be kept in mind that this title did not exclusively designate the heads of the Roman Church until the ninth century, at the earliest."[7] Another author, Bob Curran, in his book *Unholy Popes* states "In 1073 . . . Pope Gregory VII forbade its [the term pope] use for any other cleric except the Bishop of Rome."[8]

What this points out is that the term *pope* did not become firmly attached to Rome for several hundred years. As

MacCulloch previously said, it became important to identify the term *pope* with the Roman Bishop at a time, "when [it] had become significant." What MacCulloch is saying is that there came a time when the bishop of Rome had to put his foot down and declare that the word *pope* meant only (the term was being used by other religious leaders) the bishop of Rome. Apparently, according to Curran, that was in 1073, and the bishop of Rome who made this declaration of ownership and authority was Pope Gregory VII.

Now comes the back-projection. For Gregory to make such a declaration, proof had to be offered that gave the bishops of Rome the authority to claim this appellation for themselves and only for themselves. This is when the blank begins to be filled in with some creative history, which must be defined as myth, but which the Roman Catholics define as tradition: believe it because we said it.

Here is what the apostle Paul said about tradition: "See to it that no one takes you captive through hollow and deceptive philosophy, which depends on human tradition and the basic principles of this world rather than on Christ" (Col. 2:8).

What is deceptive philosophy? Philosophy is man's reasoning that "depends on human tradition," that is on human thinking, apart from the Word of God. Paul says this kind of thinking is deceptive. The Roman Catholic religious system is human tradition and deceptive.

To deceive is to lie. It is not just myth, legend, and tradition; it is a lie.

If you are a Roman Catholic, it's time for you to ask yourself, "Have I been taken captive?" That's the purpose of deception: to take the unaware captive. If you are a seeker, beware of being taken captive.

Here is what I think Peter would say about all of this: "We did not follow cleverly invented stories when we told you about the power and coming of our Lord Jesus Christ, but we were eyewitnesses of his majesty" (2 Peter 1:16). Peter knew, as we know, cleverly invented stories eventually are exposed for what they are.

Creating history by cleverly invented stories when there is no factual history, is a major skill of Roman Catholic popes and other Roman Catholic leadership. They've been doing it for over one thousand years.

That blank space Cheetham referred to had to be filled in order to fabricate history—to create history. The Roman Catholic religious system rests upon the purported fact of Peter being the first bishop of Rome. This system also rests upon the fabricated idea that Peter passed along the keys to the kingdom to each of his successors. We will look into the issue of the keys in the next chapter.

But, for now, I hope you are convinced that the foundation stone of the Roman Catholic religious system (Peter as the bishop of Rome and the first pope) is based upon myth, legend, and ultimately comes down to deception, a lie.

The implosion continues.

CHAPTER 4

PETER: THE ROCK, THE KEYS, AND THE REALITY

IN THE TWO previous chapters, we looked at Peter as he was revealed to us before the resurrection of Jesus, and we also saw him in action through the first half of the book of Acts and in a few places in Paul's letters.

In the Gospels, Peter was an impetuous follower of Jesus seemingly a cut above the other disciples. We viewed him in several situations where he was always the first of the apostles to speak out, but also the apostle who consistently could not follow through to a satisfactory finish. His notable failure was denying Jesus three times on the night of the trial and betrayal of Jesus.

In the book of Acts and related Scriptures, Peter comes across as a strong and leading spokesman and interpreter of the Holy Spirit's actions in the early days of the birth of Christianity. He was a reporter of the Holy Spirit's wonderful work among the new believers.

Peter had the gift of healing and went about with the apostle John and in some situations by himself, healing, evangelizing, and encouraging hundreds of new believers in Christ. In fact, it is evident the Holy Spirit was using not just Peter but some of the other apostles and even some disciples by doing "wonders" and "signs" through these men.

The Christian church was getting off to a dramatic start from the original center of activity in and around Jerusalem. However, Jesus, before he ascended into heaven, charged the apostles, "But you will receive power when the Holy Spirit comes on you; and you will be my witnesses in Jerusalem, and in all Judea and Samaria, and to the ends of the earth" (Acts 1:8). Going to the "ends of the earth" begins to happen early in the history of the church.

It is not Peter who spearheads the movement of the gospel to those uttermost parts; it is primarily a new apostle named Paul who is given this responsibility.

Paul and Peter end up being at cross purposes because Peter is unable to rid himself of the religious baggage of Judaism, that is, the law of Moses. To the Jew (Peter was a Jew) all non-Jews were unclean and were referred to as Gentiles. Gentiles were unclean because they didn't follow the law of Moses (certain religious rules) but particularly the rite of circumcision. A Jew couldn't even sit down at a meal with a Gentile.

For whatever reasons, Peter couldn't let go of his Gentile prejudice. It ended up causing a serious rift between Paul and Peter. It ended up causing Peter to be restricted (in a sense) to preaching to Jews only. The rift was so serious it caused Paul to call Peter a hypocrite and an implied coward.

Ironically, after Peter defends Paul and Barnabas' ministry to Gentiles before the other apostles and elders at a council in Jerusalem, Peter disappears from the story as told in Acts. Peter is not mentioned in the major outreach of the gospel to the Gentiles. He is mentioned in one significant role, but we will come to that later.

Now, this catches our attention (his withdrawal from the record in Acts), because we remember that in the gospel of Matthew, Jesus made a remarkable statement to Peter. The statement came out of a time when Jesus asked the disciples: "Who do people say the Son of Man is?" They replied, "Some say John the Baptist; others say Elijah; and still others, Jeremiah or one of the prophets." "But what about you?" he asked. "Who do you say I am?"

Simon Peter answered, "You are the Christ, the Son of the living God." Jesus replied, "Blessed are you, Simon son of Jonah, for this was not revealed to you by man, but by my Father in heaven. And I tell you that you are Peter, and on this rock I will build my church, and the gates of Hades will not overcome it. I will give you the keys of the kingdom of heaven; whatever you bind on earth will be bound in heaven, and whatever you loose on earth will be loosed in heaven" (Matt. 16:13b–19).

It is upon these words to Peter that Roman Catholics base and justify their entire religious system. It is from this passage, over hundreds of years, the Roman Catholics have constantly and consistently claimed their right to rule the widespread and diverse world of Christianity.

In the last two chapters, we saw that Peter was never looked upon by his fellow apostles as the world leader of Christianity from a throne in Rome. We also saw that Peter was very likely never even in Rome, much less the bishop (pope) of Rome.

However, the ideas of the rock and the keys loom so large in the structure of Roman Catholicism and these concepts are tied so tightly to Peter being the first pope, that they must be explained as to their true meaning.

From Matthew 16, quoted above, we need to have a general understanding of the dialogue between Jesus and these disciples, which included Peter.

When Jesus asked "Who do people say the Son of Man is?" the question was addressed to all of the disciples. It says in verse 14, "They replied . . ." So the response to Jesus' question was a collective response: they replied.

Then Jesus asked this question, "But what about you?" Obviously Jesus was addressing this question to the *they*, the collective group. Who responded? Yes, it was the outspoken disciple, Peter. We must realize that Peter, as in many other occasions, was responding to Jesus' question on behalf of the group. This is implied from the general context of the dialogue, and it is characteristic of Peter in a number of other situations.

However, Peter's response to this second question seems to be a personal belief (not necessarily a collective belief) because of the way Jesus directly and personally responded to Peter's answer. Jesus replied: "Blessed are you, Simon son of Jonah, for this was not revealed to you by man, but by my Father in heaven. And I tell you that you are Peter, and on this rock [Peter's name means rock] I will build my church, and the gates of Hades will not overcome it" (Matt. 16:17–18).

Now we must understand that Jesus would never declare a human being the rock upon which he would build his church. It is abundantly clear beginning in the Old Testament that the "rock" is always identified in a personal way as God, and in the New Testament, as Jesus. Following are two examples. "So Moses took the staff from the LORD's presence, just as he commanded him. He and Aaron gathered the assembly together in front of the rock and Moses said to them, 'Listen, you rebels, must we bring you water out of this rock?'" Then Moses raised his arm and struck the rock twice with his staff. Water gushed out, and the community and their livestock drank" (Num. 20:9–11).

The verse above is interpreted for us by the apostle Paul in 1 Corinthians, as follows: "For I do not want you to be ignorant of the fact, brothers, that our forefathers were all under the cloud and that they all passed through the sea. They were all baptized into Moses in the cloud and in the sea. They all ate the same spiritual food and drank the same spiritual drink; for they drank from the spiritual rock that accompanied them, and that rock was Christ" (1 Cor. 10:1–4).

Paul says definitively and clearly, "and that rock was Christ." If you looked at all the references in the Old Testament to where the word *rock* appears, you would find an abundance of listings where it is connected to God and to Christ.

Besides the above, here is one more connection between the Old Testament and the New Testament that specifically points to Jesus as the rock of both the Old and New Testaments. Romans 9:33 that follows is a combination quote from Isaiah 8:14 and 28:16. "As it is written: "See, I lay in Zion a stone that causes men to stumble and a rock that makes them fall, and *the one who trusts in him will never be put to shame*" (Rom. 9:33).

In the next chapter, Romans 10, Paul connects the stone (rock) to Jesus: "That if you confess with your mouth, 'Jesus is Lord,' and believe in your heart that God raised him from the dead, you will be saved. For it is with your heart that you believe and are justified, and it is with your mouth that you confess and are saved. As the Scripture says, *'Anyone who trusts in him will never be put to shame'*" (Rom. 10:9–11).

The italicization in the verses just quoted is supplied by this author for the purpose of making sure the reader gets the connection that the stone and rock of Romans 9:33, Isaiah 8:14, and 28:16 are the same as the Jesus of Romans 10:9–11.

So what do we conclude when Jesus said, "On this rock I will build my church"? Did Jesus mean a human being like Peter was the rock? From the above quotes and explanations, it is clear Jesus would never have meant that Peter, himself, was the rock. As many Bible students have concluded, Jesus was referring to Peter's statement, "You are the Christ, the Son of the Living God."

It was upon this fundamental truth (this rock) of who Jesus is that the church would be built. This truth is the "stumbling stone" upon which many people stumble, fall, and whose unbelief points them to hell. The word *stumble* in Romans 9:33 means to, "strike at; to surge against."[1]

Parenthetically, to stumble when faced with the truth of who Jesus is, is not a passive response. It is a negative response and means the one who stumbles has a bad attitude toward Jesus and will act out against Jesus because he doesn't believe Jesus is the Son of the Living God, and his/her Savior.

The only conclusion we can come to is that Peter was not the rock upon which Jesus would build his church. The rock was Peter's confession of who Jesus is, and that confession was not of Peter's own understanding, but was given to him to declare at that time by the Father.

The entire Roman Catholic religious structure and belief system rests upon the false doctrine that Peter was the rock upon which Jesus would build his church. That doctrine is clearly heretical.

And what about the keys? Jesus also said to Peter: "I will give you the keys of the kingdom of heaven; whatever you bind on earth will be bound in heaven, and whatever you loose on earth will be loosed in heaven" (Matt. 16:19).

First of all, we must note that in every other reference to keys in the two testaments, Old and New, where a person is involved, the word *keys* is either indirectly or specifically referring to Jesus.

For example, in Isaiah this is said of Jesus: "For to us a child is born, to us a son is given, and the government will be on his shoulders. And he will be called Wonderful Counselor, Mighty God, Everlasting Father, Prince of Peace. Of the increase of his government and peace there will be no end. He will reign on David's throne and over his kingdom" (Isa. 9:6–7).

When the text says, "the government will be on his shoulders," it signifies that he will have the key to the government placed on his shoulders. This is an allusion to a practice in the Old Testament. There is no question that the above text from Isaiah chapter 9 is a reference to Jesus. In the next text, we can see this practice referred to and that the key to the house of David is involved. "In that day I will summon my servant, Eliakim, son of Hilkiah. I will clothe him with your robe and fasten your sash around him and hand your authority over to him. He will be a father to those who live in Jerusalem and to the house of Judah. I will place on his shoulder the key to the house of David; what he opens no one can shut, and what he shuts no one can open" (Isa. 22:20–22).

Even though in the text just quoted, a person, Eliakim is named, this is a prophecy and Isaiah is using the name of a former palace administrator and ancestor[2] of Jesus to refer to the coming administrator who will also have "the key on his shoulder." That coming person is clearly identified when the text says that he will have the "key to the house of David," and it also says "what he opens no one can shut, and what he shuts no one can open."

These texts are not referring to Peter. In the following text, it is specifically stated who has the key to the house to David, and "what he opens no one can shut, and what he shuts no one can open." The text is in italics so the reader can keep track of these closely aligned statements in all of these texts. "To the angel of the church in Philadelphia write: These are the words of him who is holy and true, who holds the key of David. *What he opens no one can shut, and what he shuts no one can open*" (Rev. 3:7).

While interpreting and understanding this issue of the keys, it is important to observe that there are other places in the New Testament where it is applied to the other disciples, not just Peter, and is extended to include forgiveness of sins, church discipline, and answers to prayer.

In Matthew 18:18, we read (italics for emphasis): "I tell you the truth, *whatever you bind on earth will be bound in heaven, and whatever you loose on earth will be loosed in heaven.*"

In the context of Jesus' statement, as taken from Matthew 18:1, Jesus is answering questions brought to him from the disciples, and he does some teaching that goes beyond the questions.

In the passage quoted below, Jesus is teaching the disciples first about forgiveness, church discipline, and answers to prayer.

> If your brother sins against you, go and show him his fault, just between the two of you. If he listens to you, you have won your brother over. But if he will not listen, take one or two others along, so that "every matter may be established by the testimony of two or three witnesses." If he refuses to listen to them, tell it to the church; and if he refuses to listen even to the church, treat him as you would a pagan or a tax collector. *I tell you the truth, whatever you bind on earth will be bound in heaven, and whatever you loose on earth will be*

loosed in heaven. Again, I tell you that if two of you on earth agree about anything you ask for, it will be done for you by my Father in heaven. For where two or three come together in my name, there am I with them (Matt. 18:15–20).

The italicized portion in the text above was done by this author to help the reader observe the significance of this text in this particular passage and as this text relates to the other similar texts that are italicized.

Who is Jesus talking to in the above Scripture? It said in chapter 18, verse 1, "At that time the disciples came to Jesus and asked . . ." Who are these disciples? We don't really know, but in many references in the Gospels it meant the group of people who were following Jesus at that time. In other words, Jesus spoke these words about binding and loosing to a group that likely consisted of more than just the inner circle, but he certainly spoke them to at least the Twelve. The point is that these words were not spoken to Peter alone.

There is another passage where Jesus speaks words that are similar in intent (italics for emphasis). "Again Jesus said, 'Peace be with you! As the Father has sent me, I am sending you.' And with that he breathed on them and said, 'Receive the Holy Spirit. *If you forgive anyone his sins, they are forgiven; if you do not forgive them, they are not forgiven*'" (John 20:21–23).

Again, we read that these words with similar meaning, although not exactly the same words as in Matthew 16, were spoken to others besides Peter. In this particular place and time, we don't know who or how many disciples heard these words. It is notable that in verse 24 of this passage, the terms *the Twelve* and *disciples* are spoken of in a way that indicates the Twelve were part of a larger group.

So, who really has the keys? And what were the keys? I don't think we can really answer those questions without exploring the book of Acts. It is in the beginning chapters of Acts where the significance and meaning of the keys is demonstrated in the real life and actions of the apostles, particularly of Peter, but also in other apostles and believers.

It is also in Acts that we clearly see who the rock is upon whom the church is being built, and it is not Peter or any other apostle.

It is important to note that the words *rock* and *keys* are never mentioned by anyone in the book of Acts. None of the other apostles, specifically in Acts, or in any of their writings ever uses these two terms as referring to Peter. After the Gospels, the rock and the keys disappear from the vocabulary of the apostles and other believers.

John, in the book of Revelation, refers to Jesus and angels having keys for certain activities. But, again, Peter has no connection to these statements.

Besides the other apostles, Peter doesn't even refer to these concepts as regarding himself, either directly or in an oblique way, with one exception. But even in the exception, he doesn't use the words *rock* or *keys*.

What is that exception? It occurs at the time when Peter got up in front of the apostles and elders in Jerusalem to defend Paul and Barnabas. As you will recall, Paul and Barnabas were in Jerusalem to report to the apostles and elders about their ministry to the Gentiles. There was a heated discussion as some Jewish believers didn't want to recognize Gentile believers as legitimate members of the body of Christ. So, we find Peter defending them by explaining his own experience preaching to a Gentile named Cornelius. That story is in Acts, chapter 10.

Peter's defense of Paul and Barnabas is recorded this way in chapter 15: "After much discussion, Peter got up and addressed them: 'Brothers, you know that some time ago God made a choice among you that the Gentiles might hear from my lips the message of the gospel and believe. God who knows the heart, showed that he accepted them by giving the Holy Spirit to them, just as he did to us'" (Acts 15:7–8).

This is the only reference in Acts, or any other Scripture except the passages in the Gospels which we have already looked at, where Peter makes reference to having had a special role in laying the foundation of the Christian church.

Recognize, too, that Peter was undeniably withdrawn from a ministry to the Gentiles as we learned in an earlier chapter. We can only conclude that when God made a choice for the Gentiles to hear the gospel from Peter's lips, God meant for Peter to be the first (the first but not the only one) of the apostles to tell the Gentiles about Jesus and the Holy Spirit.

His words were, "God made a choice among you that the Gentiles might hear from my lips the message of the gospel and believe." That's it. There is no reference to being the rock or having the keys. Why not? Because he wasn't the rock, and he didn't possess the keys in an absolute sense as the Roman Catholics would have the world to believe.

However, that is not *it* when we observe some other actions of Peter in the early days of the church. If we read and think carefully about what occurred and how Peter was involved in those early days, we can see just what Jesus meant when he said Peter had the keys.

According to the NIV Compact Dictionary of the Bible, the word *key(s)* symbolizes authority.[3] Obviously, a key also locks and unlocks something. In the passages in the New Testament we have looked at where the word *key* is used, the meaning always emphasizes authority. In other Scriptures, the word often refers to the utility of locking and unlocking. Both meanings, then, were brought together by Jesus in the use of the word *keys*—authority and utility.

Not only was Peter given the authority to use the keys, but as he used his authority, great truths would be first announced by him to a waiting world. As it were, great truths about Jesus and the Holy Spirit were opened to those who believed and closed to those who rejected these truths. Heaven was opened and closed depending on the response.

On two occasions in Acts, chapter 1, Jesus, before his ascension into heaven, promised the disciples that they would "be baptized with the Holy Spirit" and that they would "receive power when the Holy Spirit comes on you" (Acts 1:5, 8).

The coming of the Holy Spirit was a key to the opening of the hearts of mankind to believe in the Lord Jesus Christ. And who had that key? Who announced the coming of the Holy Spirit? None other than Peter.

It happened on the day of Pentecost. A group of disciples were gathered at a house. "Suddenly a sound like the blowing of a violent wind came from heaven and filled the whole house where they were sitting. They saw what seemed to be tongues of fire that separated and came to rest on each of them. All of them were filled with the Holy Spirit and began to speak in other tongues as the Spirit enabled them" (Acts 2:2–4).

There was a large group of people in Jerusalem for this feast day of the Jews: the day of Pentecost. Many of these people heard the sound coming from the house where the disciples were being filled with the Holy Spirit and speaking in tongues. They were amazed at what they were hearing because every one of the crowd was hearing the "praises of God" in his own language. They were "amazed and perplexed," they asked one another, "What does this mean?" (Acts 2:12). "Then Peter stood up with the Eleven [notice that all the apostles stood up, but only Peter spoke], raised his voice and addressed the crowd. . . . This is what was spoken by the prophet Joel: 'In the last days, God says, I will pour out my Spirit on all people. . . . And everyone who calls on the name of the Lord will be saved'" (Acts 2:14–21).

Peter exercised the authority given to him by Jesus to open up to the men present on that day of Pentecost the coming of the Holy Spirit. Peter opened their understanding and gave them the knowledge they needed to answer their question, "What does this mean?"

It's good to remember that in this instance of Peter's exercising his authority and presenting the Holy Spirit to these men, they were all Jews. But, we must remember, too, that Peter unlocked and opened the gospel to the Gentiles as well, as he said in Acts 15:7, "Brothers, you know that some time ago God made a choice among you that the Gentiles might hear from my lips the message of the gospel and believe."

When Jesus gave Peter the keys, note that it was plural; there was more than one key. What is the second key? As we follow along in chapter 2 of Acts, we will see that a second key was necessary to open the door of understanding of this Jewish group and to fully answer their question, "What does this mean?"

Peter went on to tell this group of men (Jewish men from all over that region of the world, including Africa, Egypt, Mesopotamia, and even Rome) about another truth that had been hidden behind closed doors for centuries. For the Jews, the coming of Jesus (the Messiah, Christ—Savior) and the Holy Spirit were promises that had not yet been fulfilled. It was given to Peter to be the first to announce that the promise of Jesus and the Holy Spirit was now fulfilled. The apostle Paul put it this way: "But when the time had fully come, God sent his Son, born of a woman, born under law, to redeem those under law, that we might receive the full rights of sons. Because you are sons, God sent the Spirit of his Son into our hearts, the Spirit who calls out "*Abba*, Father." So you are no longer a slave, but a son; and since you are a son, God has made you also an heir" (Gal. 4:4–7).

In addition, prior to the quote above, Paul said: "Before this faith came, we were held prisoners by the law, locked up until faith should be revealed" (Gal. 3:23).

So, the keys (Jesus and the Holy Spirit—their utility) unlocked us from the law which required that we be totally righteous: We couldn't free ourselves from the law's requirements; we couldn't satisfy the righteous demands of God as expressed in the law of Moses.

Peter put it this way:

"Men of Israel, listen to this: Jesus of Nazareth was a man accredited by God to you by miracles, wonders and signs, which God did among you through him, as you yourselves know. This man was handed over to you by God's set purpose and foreknowledge; and you, with the help of wicked men, put him to death by nailing him to the cross. But God raised him from the dead, freeing him from the agony of death, because it was impossible for death to keep its hold on him. . . . God has raised this Jesus to life, and we are all witnesses of the fact. Exalted to the right hand of God, he has received from the Father the promised Holy Spirit, and has poured out what you now see and hear. . . . Therefore, let all Israel be assured of this: God has made this Jesus, whom you crucified, both Lord and Christ." When the people heard this, they were cut to the heart and said to Peter and the other apostles, "Brothers, what shall we do?" (Acts 2:22–37)

The first question this crowd asked was, "What does this mean?" Peter, with the eleven other apostles standing up with him, began to explain the meaning of the Holy Spirit's coming. Then Peter explained about Jesus' death, resurrection, and ascension to the right hand of the Father. At the end of the explanation about Jesus, Peter said, "God has made this Jesus, whom you crucified, both Lord and Christ."

Then, the crowd asked, "Brothers, what shall we do?"

Peter responded: "Repent and be baptized, every one of you, in the name of Jesus Christ for the forgiveness of your sins. And you will receive the gift of the Holy Spirit" (Acts 2:38).

There they are, the keys: Jesus and the Holy Spirit. The keys to what? Peter opened the door of salvation to this crowd of Jewish men through applying the keys of Jesus and the Holy Spirit. But that door (heaven's door) would be closed to some: those who didn't repent and refused to be identified with Jesus and the Holy Spirit through the act of baptism.

The Roman Catholics claim that Peter was the only one with these keys, that he was the bishop of Rome, that he handed the keys off to the next bishop of Rome, and that this has been going on for centuries. It means that every pope from Peter (supposedly) on to the present time possessed the keys, and only that pope (that bishop of Rome) had the keys to the kingdom of heaven.

They exalt Peter above all the other apostles and every Christian who has ever lived. They call this the *primacy* of Peter. They, then, extend this primacy to mean that the current pope has primacy over every other Christian leader in the whole wide world. Webster's dictionary defines primacy as, "the state of being first (as in importance, order, or rank)."

The Roman Catholics call this handing on of the keys, *succession*. In practical, up-to-date terms, it means that the current pope, Francis, has these keys and he is the only one who has them. It means no other Christian can have these keys, only Pope Francis, and the Roman Catholic bishops and priests whom the pope acknowledges and ordains.

Again, in practical terms, it means that only Pope Francis or a Roman Catholic priest can open or shut the kingdom of God to an individual. It means that you must be baptized by water as a Roman Catholic in order to be saved; that is, you must go to a Roman Catholic Church and participate in their religious rites and rituals to be a Christian, because only they have the keys to the kingdom of heaven. Only the Roman Catholics can let you in, or keep you out of heaven.

It has already been shown in previous chapters that Peter had no primacy over the other apostles, that he had no authority to give the keys to anyone else (and didn't ever do such a thing), and that he was never the bishop of Rome.

But, it would also be good for us to see how the keys were actually passed out to several others, and Peter had nothing to do with this distribution. In other words, succession from one bishop of Rome to another is a total myth and a heretical teaching and dogma. We will consider three examples: Stephen, Philip, and Paul.

We will see that everyone who was evangelizing in the name of Jesus had the Holy Spirit's power and blessing present with them: the keys to the kingdom of heaven.

Stephen was not an apostle. As one of the first Christians, his entire story is told in Acts, chapters 6 and 7. Stephen was one of the men chosen to wait on tables: a servant to help feed the growing crowd of believers and to make sure each got his share of the food. Then we find him as, "a man full of God's grace and power, [who] did great wonders and miraculous signs among the people" (Acts 6:8).

You might already know that Stephen ran into a lot of opposition from the Jewish leaders who weren't believers. They brought him before the Sanhedrin (this is all in chapter 6) to be tried for blasphemy. Chapter 7 is Stephen's response, his defense, which so angered the Jewish leaders that they determined to kill him—to have him stoned to death.

During the process of stoning, as Stephen was dying, these words are recorded: "But Stephen, full of the Holy Spirit, looked up to heaven and saw the glory of God, and Jesus standing at the right hand of God. 'Look,' he said, 'I see heaven open and the Son of Man standing at the right hand of God'" (Acts 7:55–56).

Can we deny that Stephen, full of the Holy Spirit, preaching Jesus, doing miraculous signs and wonders and dying for his faith, also had the keys to the kingdom? Peter had nothing to do with Stephen's ministry. There is no mention of Peter's handing on the keys to Stephen. It was the Holy Spirit's presence and power in Stephen that put him in position to preach the gospel and ultimately to die for his faith.

Philip was another of the seven men chosen to wait on tables. We find him as another witness who possessed the keys, and his story is in Acts, chapter 8. "Those who had been scattered [due to persecution] preached the word wherever they went. [Note: all of these displaced believers preached the word.] Philip went down to a city in Samaria and proclaimed the Christ there. When the crowds heard Philip and saw the miraculous signs he did, they all paid close attention to what he said. With shrieks, evil spirits came out of many, and many paralytics and cripples were healed. So there was great joy in that city" (Acts 8:4–8).

Once again, can anyone deny that these believers and Philip had the keys to the kingdom? And, again, Peter had nothing to do with their possessing the keys. There are other incidents in Philip's ministry that clearly reveal that Philip had the keys (Jesus and the Holy Spirit). Philip's complete ministry can be read in Acts, chapter 8.

Now we come to the apostle Paul. No doubt you know all about the salvation and calling of Paul. You know that Jesus spoke to Paul on the road to Damascus. It was a personal, miraculous intervention of Jesus in Paul's life. Following is part of the story of Paul's salvation: "But the Lord said to Ananias, 'Go! This man is my chosen instrument to carry my name before the Gentiles and their kings and before the people of Israel. . . . Then Ananias went to the house and entered it. Placing his hands on Saul, he said, 'Brother Saul, the Lord—Jesus, who appeared to you on the road as you were coming here—has sent me so that you may see again and be filled with the Holy Spirit'" (Acts 9:15–17).

The reason for telling of these three ministers of the gospel—as they administered the keys (Jesus and the Holy Spirit)—is to show that Peter had nothing to do with their selection to be ministers of the gospel. Peter did not hand over the keys to these men. They, by virtue of their personal salvation, spiritual gifts, and leading of the Holy Spirit, had the keys and opened the door of salvation to many others.

That process of personal relationship to Jesus through believing in him and the subsequent presence and power of the Holy Spirit in their lives, made them possessors of the keys. They had the keys within themselves.

Listen, there is no *scriptural* record of Peter's supposed role of having to hand on the keys to anyone else, much less the title of bishop of Rome. If you are a believer, you have the keys within yourself. You can't be a believer in Jesus and not have the keys because Jesus and the Holy Spirit are the keys.

As the apostle Paul said, "Christ in you, the hope of glory" (Col. 1:27), and who also said "And if anyone does not have the Spirit of Christ, he does not belong to Christ" (Rom. 8:9b).

Neither Peter, the bishops of Rome (past and present), nor anyone else, had or has had anything to do with a person's getting into the kingdom of heaven in the manner the Roman Catholics propagate.

It is true that Jesus gave Peter the opportunity to be the first apostle to open the eyes of the Jews and the Gentiles to the coming of the Holy Spirit and the death, resurrection, and ascension into heaven of Jesus, their Messiah and Savior. But, as has been shown, every apostle had those keys, and from that point on, every believer has the keys within themselves.

That's the reality and the truth of the rock and the keys.

The apostle Paul said: "By the grace God has given me, I laid a foundation as an expert builder, and someone else is building on it. But each one should be careful how he builds. For no one can lay any foundation other than the one already laid, which is Jesus Christ" (1 Cor. 3:10–11).

Paul also said: "Consequently, you are no longer foreigners and aliens, but fellow citizens with God's people and members of God's household, built on the foundation of the apostles and prophets, with Christ Jesus himself as the chief cornerstone" (Eph. 2:19–20).

Peter said of himself: "To the elders among you, I appeal as fellow elder" (1 Peter 5:1).

Peter never declared himself to be anything but a fellow elder.

Jesus the Christ is the only foundation, not Peter and the succession of popes, nor the Roman Catholic Church. Who laid this foundation? Paul told us it was the apostles and prophets.

Note that those two appellations are plural. It was not one apostle (as in Peter), nor any one prophet. It didn't even begin with the apostles but with the prophets of the Old Testament.

In the next chapter, we will see just what confusion, distortion, and contradiction this Roman Catholic heresy produced in the long chain of popes, which was anonymously called, "a rope of sand."

Not only was the foundation rock nonexistent, but the rope was incredibly faulty and broken in so many places that the Roman Catholic religion could not stand under the scrutiny of the Scriptures.

An implosion is coming. The scriptural charges are being set.

CHAPTER FIVE

THE DUBIOUS HISTORY OF POPERY

THERE ARE SO many books written about the history of Christianity that a person could spend a lifetime researching this topic. They all tell the same basic story. It does depend upon whether you are reading a Catholic author, a secular author, or an author who identifies himself as neutral.

I noted, too, that some authors, while knowing the unaccredited nature of the history of Roman Catholicism, do not bring this hoax to judgment. In my view, many authors, while knowing the truth, enable the Roman Catholic religion to escape historical censor. Interestingly, it is secular writers who reveal the true nature of Catholicism more often than religious historians who are Catholic or who are, for some reason, friendly to Catholicism.

Because I don't speak or read any language other than English, I was limited in my selection to secondary and sometimes tertiary authors: books written in English, some being translations. However, I did seek to choose authors who have legitimate reputations for being good historians.

It was difficult to find unbiased authors. Some fell into the subjective trap Joseph Ayer points out in the following comment: "An author may not be conscious of any attempt to make his selection of texts illustrate or support any particular phase of Christian belief or ecclesiastical polity, and his one aim may be to treat the matter objectively and to render his book useful to all, yet he ought not to flatter himself that in either respect he has been entirely successful."[1]

Yes, you might consider me biased. However, if I am biased, it is only on the basis of the Bible as the only Word of God and on the basis of authentic history. I own up to that bias.

Catholic authors in this generation, are particularly candid about their religious experience and the history from which it has grown. The ones I read, especially post-Vatican II authors, seemed to be in the midst of major changes in their thinking, and I would say even seem to be experiencing confusion about Catholicism and their personal experience in Catholicism. Many doubt the efficacy of the papacy and some doubt Mary's ascendancy. And actually, if we look back, doubters can be found all through the history of Catholicism. But, contemporary authors continue, for the most part, to defend their Catholic religion.

In this chapter, I'm going to be quite selective in the quotes used. But you can be assured you would find these statements, in general, in all honest histories of Christianity, even most Catholic histories. The facts are irrefutable. Unfortunately, enabling is an unhappy characteristic of some authors.

The word *enabling* means, for example, just as wives or husbands might refuse to admit the alcoholism of their spouse and seek to cover up the addiction with friends and family, so do some historians enable Catholicism by covering up or explaining away discrepancies and contradictions with the Bible. Therefore, any seeker of the truth must be aware of whose work they are reading and what the author's personal stake in the story might be. Did the author enable the myths of Catholicism, or is he candid and tells the complete unvarnished story? Does the author pass any judgment on what he is writing about; Catholic historians do not. Perhaps historians are not supposed to pass judgment.

From the previous three chapters of this book, it is clear and without controversy that the Scriptures, the Bible, gives no credence to the notion that Peter was the first bishop of Rome and, therefore, the first pope. The idea of a pope who rules all of Christianity from a throne in Rome is without merit, a hoax. It is true, however, that millions of people over several hundred years have believed this hoax.

Even today, as I write, Pope Francis is roaming around the world (with a stop in the United States) masquerading as the Vicar of Christ: the representative of Jesus the Christ here on this earth. The sad and terrible reality is that millions of people, including heads of many governments, treat him as the Vicar of Christ. Some even bow to him and kiss his ring.

Can you imagine any of the apostles, especially Peter or Paul, wearing the clothing that Catholic popes and priests wear and allowing anyone to bow to them or to kiss their hands or feet? Would they have allowed anyone to call them Father? I hope you've read enough of the New Testament to shudder at the thought.

If you are not convinced from the previous chapters of this book that the concept of a pope as the personal and infallible representative of Christ is a hoax, perhaps the following sketch of the lives and actions of many of the popes will convince you that Jesus would never have appointed these men to represent him.

First of all, we must realize the concept of a succession of popes took many years to develop. There were many ups and downs over those years. It is not a pretty picture; it is "the good, the bad, and the ugly." As the anonymous author from the past said, "It is a rope of sand."

The person who characterized the popes as a rope of sand was using the analogy of a rope to mean what is called succession in the Roman Catholic religion. Succession, in the Catholic context, refers to the long chain of popes from Peter forward who inherited Peter's keys; the keys to the kingdom of heaven. This means that every subsequent pope after Peter, according to Catholic teaching, has the keys to the kingdom of heaven.

By Catholic reasoning, the current pope, Pope Francis, has the keys. This means Pope Francis is the current Vicar of Christ and determines, by the rules and rites he proclaims and supports, who will get into heaven, or not; he has the keys.

As you will see in the next pages, succession is a rope of sand. Pope Francis is out on the end of that rope. That's akin to being out on the end of a limb that is being sawed off.

Anyone who builds his/her religious experience and hopes upon Peter, the popes, and the Catholic religion is building on sand. As Jesus warned us: "Therefore, everyone who hears these words of mine and puts them into practice is like a wise man who built his house on the rock. The rain came down, the streams rose, and the winds blew and beat against that house; yet it did not fall, because it had its foundation on the rock. But everyone who hears these words of mine and does not put them into practice is like a foolish man who built his house on sand" (Matt. 7:24–26).

Jesus' words constitute the rock. It is not the words of a bishop (pope), priest, or anyone else. Everything else is sand. In the case of succession, it is merely a rope of sand: a myth, and a hoax.

As was shown in the previous chapters of this book, Jesus and the Holy Spirit are the keys to the kingdom of heaven, and every true believer in Christ has the keys within himself.

Now we must remember that the persons we will look at in this chapter all claimed to be the Vicar of Christ: the personal and complete and only representative of Jesus the Christ, the Son of the Living God. Each one was supposedly the rock upon which Jesus built (and is building) his church, and each one, in succession, had the keys to the kingdom.

If you have any doubts about whether this is a hoax, a masquerade, be sure to read at least the gospel of John in the New Testament. That is, if the following account doesn't convince you that these men were not the personal representatives of Jesus here on earth, read John's gospel. Surely you will see the contradiction and realize that it is all a hoax by reading who Jesus was, what he said and did, and who he said would follow him as his one and only, personal representative here on earth: the Holy Spirit.

I'm not saying that there aren't gifted (gifted by the Holy Spirit) men and women who take leadership roles in the churches, but they are not monarchical, that is, rulers over other men and women with the same gifts as in ruling over other bishops: bishops weren't meant to become popes.

How did the concept of a pope begin? The following is only a brief sketch of the historical background of popery. Several of the books in the bibliography would provide anyone wanting to pursue this topic with ample, and in some cases, detailed information about the lives of many of the popes.

In the early days of Christianity, as the gospel of Christ was preached and taught throughout the then known world, certain men in some notable cities believed in and received Jesus into their lives. As time went on, some of these men became what was called *bishops*. They became bishops of these notable cities.

For example, there were bishops in Jerusalem, Antioch, Rome, Alexandria in Egypt, and Carthage in North Africa. Some scholars say there was more than one bishop in Rome. If true, that alone brings the whole scheme down in pieces.

If you read the history of the birth of Christianity and the subsequent birth of Roman Catholicism, the picture becomes clear. The ruling bishops in the various notable cities seemed to choose the bishop of Rome as the most significant bishop. The following overview is quite sketchy, but the broad picture is accurate.

It started with a letter that Clement, the then bishop of Rome, wrote to the church in Corinth.[2] In this letter, Clement really gets on the case of the believers in Corinth. Clement's letter has a lot of the same disciplinary attitude as Paul had when writing the books of 1 and 2 Corinthians.

Some of the other bishops of the notable cities received copies of Clement's letter. They liked how Clement stepped up and scolded the Corinthians. And they felt it was particularly appropriate for Clement to be the one to do this as he was the bishop of Rome; Rome being the most important (powerful and prestigious) of the notable cities.

Over time, one thing led to another, as the saying goes, and the bishops of Rome began to assert their right to be the arbiter of doctrinal disputes (called *heresies*) and other issues pertaining to the establishment and growth of Christianity.

Parenthetically, it is highly ironic to note that the bishops of Rome became the key guardians of what was considered orthodox beliefs, battled the heretics who proposed alternate beliefs, but, then over time, the bishops of Rome developed a religion that became the greatest heresy (regarding Christianity) the religious world had and has ever known.

Many of the other bishops of notable cities either totally succumbed to the bishops of Rome, or kind of halfheartedly succumbed. The bishops of Constantinople, in particular, totally resisted the notion that the bishops of Rome were the worldwide leaders of Christianity (the popes), and, in fact, laid claim to that role themselves. The bishop of Rome eventually won the battle.

The whole process was quite complicated and would require another book to explain. There are already so many books that detail the process of the bishops of Rome battling for their preeminence (the recognition of the bishop of Rome as the pope and czar of all Christianity—the Vicar of Christ) that another book is not necessary. For the purposes of this book, a broad outline is all that will be presented.

Actually, and this is extremely important, none of the bishops in the early years of Christianity considered themselves as Vicars of Christ. Nicolas Cheetham explains and defines the technical term *bishop* as follows: "Roman bishops regarded themselves neither as the vicars of Christ nor as the exclusive wielders of apostolic authority. The word *episkopos* had originally no priestly significance; it was used in a purely administrative context and meant supervisor or steward. The *episkopos* of an early Christian community seems normally to have been assisted by a council of presbyters or elders, a small group of older and experienced men. They too exercised no priestly functions in the modern sense but served as advisers or teachers."[3]

There is a meaningful discrepancy between the above definition and how the role of bishop is defined in NIV Compact Dictionary of the Bible. "The title 'elder' or 'presbyter' generally applied to the same man; 'elder' referring to his age and dignity, and 'bishop' to his work of superintendence."[4]

Note how Cheetham separated the concept of bishop into two distinct roles: supervisor as one distinct role and presbyters (elders) as another distinct role. Cheetham's definition is erroneous as born out in Archibald Robertson's, *Word Pictures in the New Testament* and as already cited from the NIV Dictionary.

Robertson makes this statement in his commentary on 1 Timothy 3:2: "The word [*The bishop (ton episkopon)*] does not in the N.T. have the monarchical sense found in Ignatius [The role of Ignatius is explained later] of a bishop over elders."[5]

What is meant by "monarchical sense?" Robertson makes it clear that in the meaning of the word *bishop*, there is no justification for doing as the Catholics have done (and Cheetham did) by dividing the word into two distinct roles (or persons); one bishop as the ruler over the other bishops. Robertson cited Ignatius as Ignatius was one of the early church leaders who contributed to the concept of a ruling bishop, which later morphed into the concept of popery.

Because this word *bishop* is so significant in the evolution of the monarchical concept that developed (note *monarchical* is derived from the word *monarch*), the following is one more interpretation provided to reinforce the true meaning of the word bishop. This is from Vine's *Expository Dictionary of New Testament Words:* "Note: Presbuteros, an elder, is another term for the same person as bishop or overseer. . . . The term "elder" indicates the mature spiritual experience and understanding of those so described; the term "bishop," or "overseer," indicates the character of the work undertaken . . . there were to be bishops in every local church."[6]

Vine makes the points that a bishop and an elder were the same person and that bishops were to be in every local church. This is such a significant concept that we must examine the situation more closely because popery was a direct result of this monarchical heresy.

The concept of monarchical bishop was pushed distinctly and personally by Ignatius. He was the bishop of Antioch (a major Gentile church northwest of Jerusalem). For some reason, he felt that he should be the bishop of several churches. Williston Walker outlined the historical antecedents and the evolution of a powerful combination of the monarchical bishopric with apostolic succession, in a manner that is easy to understand.

> One further observation of great importance is to be made. Clement of Rome (93–97) [Bishop of Rome], writing when Rome had as yet no monarchical bishop, traces the existence of church officers to apostolic succession. It is no impeachment of the firmness of his conviction, though it militates against the historic accuracy of his view, that he apparently bases it on a misunderstanding of Paul's statement in *1 Cor.* 16. On the other hand, Ignatius, though urging in the strongest terms the value of the monarchical episcopate as the bond of unity, knows nothing of an apostolical succession. It was the union of these two principles, a monarchical bishop in apostolical succession, which occurred before the middle of the second century, that immensely enhanced the dignity and power of the bishopric.[7]

Walker doesn't say it, but it immensely enhanced the dignity and power of the coming popes. It was, in fact, the traditional and theological (not biblical) basis of the power of the popes. Of course, as we already know, Peter was erroneously established (by back-filling the historical record) as the first bishop of Rome, so for Roman Catholics, everything rested on the erroneous notion that Peter was the first pope: the rock upon which Jesus would build his church.

It will be good to check in with Jesus to hear what he had to say about a process that would end up with one bishop ruling over all others. The quote that follows is Jesus' response to the mother of two of the disciples as she asked Jesus to, "grant that one of these two sons of mine may sit at your right and the other at your left in your kingdom" (Matt. 20:21).

Jesus responds: "You know that the rulers of the Gentiles lord it over them, and their high officials exercise authority over them. Not so with you. Instead, whoever wants to become great among you must be your servant, and whoever wants to be first must be your slave—just as the Son of Man did not come to be served, but to serve, and to give his life as a ransom for many" (Matt. 20:25–28).

The apostle Paul made this statement when writing to the Corinthians, "Not that we lord it over your faith, but we work with you for your joy, because it is by faith you stand firm" (2 Cor. 1:24).

Peter, also had something to say about being a bishop [elder]. While writing his letter to the church leaders in Pontus, Galatia, Cappadocia, Asia and Bithynia (1 Peter 5:1), Peter admonishes the leaders:

> To the elders among you. I appeal as a fellow elder, a witness of Christ's sufferings and one who also will share in the glory to be revealed: Be shepherds of God's flock that is under your care, serving as overseers—not because you must, but because you are willing, as God wants you to be; not greedy for money, but eager to serve; not lording it over

those entrusted to you, but being examples to the flock. And when the Chief Shepherd appears, you will receive the crown of glory that will never fade away (1 Peter 5:1–4).

Peter was writing to several individual churches, and in this portion, he was specifically addressing the leaders of those churches. Peter made it clear that he was speaking as a fellow elder." He implied that he is just another elder. He said for emphasis, "not lording it over those entrusted to you." There is absolutely no indication of Peter writing as if he were the bishop (elder) of the leaders of these five churches. There is no indication that he was writing as if there was one elder in charge of the other elder/leaders of the other four churches. Each church was being addressed as an independent entity.

It should be clear from the above explanation of the word *bishop*, that the Holy Spirit intended that a bishop be the leader of one church. There were men, as there will always be, who will desire to grasp at more power and prestige in the churches than the Holy Spirit intended for them. History is filled with examples of this in every expression of all religions and in all eras of human activity.

Before we look at the lives of the so-called successors of Peter, I want to explore the concept of priests and sacrifices from the Old and New Testaments.

It is of great significance that, as Cheetham said, that these early leaders had no priestly functions. Why is this so? Because at that time these men were following the pattern and principles laid down by the apostles which did away with the role of priest.

New Testament Christianity represented a clear cut cleavage from the Old Testament religious system: the Jewish system based upon the law of Moses (priests and sacrifices).

Peter wrote about the new system. It was based upon a new truth, a new principle: "As you come to him, the living Stone—rejected by men but chosen by God and precious to him—you also, like living stones, are being built into a spiritual house to be a holy priesthood, offering spiritual sacrifices acceptable to God through Jesus Christ" (1 Peter 2:4–5). "But you are a chosen people, a royal priesthood, a holy nation, a people belonging to God, that you may declare the praises of him who called you out of darkness into his wonderful light" (1 Peter 2:9).

No wonder the bishops of the early church did not take on the role of priest. Realizing that every believer was now a member of a royal priesthood (an actual priest before God in their own individual right), those bishops did not even conceive of claiming to be priests.

However, in time, the Roman Catholic religious system was built upon the Judaistic and Greek/Roman religious models of priests and sacrifices. This was a major error (heresy).

In the New Testament, we are informed that Jesus by his personal sacrifice on the cross became, "once for all," the final sacrifice. Following are quotes from the book of Hebrews which make abundantly clear this transition from the Old Testament system to the New Testament. I'm beginning with the concept of Jesus as the fulfillment of the role of High Priest. "Therefore, since we have a great high priest who has gone through the heavens, Jesus the Son of God, let us hold firmly to the faith we profess. For we do not have a high priest who is unable to sympathize with our weaknesses, but we have one who has been tempted in every way, just as we are—yet was without sin. Let us then approach the throne of grace with confidence, so that we may receive mercy and find grace to help us in our time of need" (Heb. 4:14–16).

There are a number of things we can learn from the above passage.

1. Jesus is the great high priest. No other priest is needed. He is a direct connection between the believer and God.
2. Jesus represents believers in heaven at the very throne of God.
3. Jesus is the High Priest who sympathizes with our faults and failures.
4. Jesus was tempted just as we are (that's why he can sympathize with us), but he remained without sin (that's why he can represent us before God).
5. Because of Jesus, we can come to God on our own (no other mediator is necessary), and we can come with confidence (no fear of rejection).
6. Jesus, the High Priest, sits on a throne of authority and power. It is a throne dominated by mercy and grace toward those who come in the right way, through Jesus the High Priest.
7. Grace and mercy mean that by coming through Jesus the High Priest, we will be the beneficiaries of God's blessing, forgiveness, and favor: his specific answers to our prayers and his watch care over us. Mercy and grace eliminate the need for penance.

In the following chapter of Hebrews, this was said of Jesus: "No one takes this honor upon himself; he must be called by God, just as Aaron was. So Christ also did not take upon himself the glory of becoming a high priest" (Heb. 5:4–5).

It is clear. There is only one High Priest—only one priest that counts—it is Jesus. And Jesus didn't choose this position.

He was appointed to it by God the Father. So we must conclude there is no such person as a human priest standing between God and man. The priests of the Roman Catholic religious system are a hoax, just as the pope is a hoax.

The early Christian followers of Jesus who were appointed by their congregations as bishops understood that they were not priests (as Cheetham noted) and never claimed that role. The very word *bishop* does not contain that meaning.

Why and how have Catholic leaders developed a religious system that includes popes/bishops/priests as the sole representatives of God on earth, and the possessors of the authority to forgive sins, and to carry out other sacerdotal functions. *Sacerdotal* means, according to Webster's, "essential mediators between God and mankind."

It must be clear to you from all that has been said up to this point in this book that there is only one mediator between God and man, and that is Jesus. It is the extreme height of impertinence and heresy for Catholic leadership to claim such a role.

Remember, too, that the Catholics themselves didn't even claim priesthood for several hundred years. That claim was an example of back-filling history—revisionist history.

As it turns out, there is one text in the book of Romans from which the Catholics base their erroneous claim to be priests. As we will see, their claim, from this one text, is a case of misinterpretation. Those who write about this method of interpretation call it proof-texting. That is, coming up with an idea and then finding a text of Scripture to support the idea.

In the case of Romans 15:16, we read, "To be a minister of Christ Jesus to the Gentiles with the priestly duty of proclaiming the gospel of God, so that the Gentiles might become an offering acceptable to God, sanctified by the Holy Spirit."

The phrase *priestly duty* is taken from this text by Catholics to infer that whenever the popes/bishops/priests perform any religious duties, these duties are acts authorized and are efficacious because they are priests.

What, in fact, did Paul mean when he wrote that "proclaiming the gospel of God" was an act of priestly duty? It does seem to mean that Paul considered preaching as an act coequal with the duties of the pagan priests, or Old Testament priests.

Did Paul mean to tell us that when he preached the gospel, he was performing a religious rite just like the priests of pagan or Old Testament religions? Was he saying that he was the he was the mediator between God and man?

Note that there are two words used in Paul's text: *minister* and *priestly*. Both words, according to *Vine's Expository Dictionary of New Testament Words*, in their fundamental meaning, express the thought of service.[8]

If Paul was referring back to the mediatorial acts of the Old Testament priests, it was only as a metaphor. Archibald Robertson in *Word Pictures in the New Testament*, says this, "But this purely metaphorical use does not show that Paul attached a 'sacerdotal' character to the ministry."[9]

The key thought from Robertson's comment is that Paul is using *priestly* as a metaphor, a word picture. Paul did not mean he was equating, in any exact correspondence, preaching the gospel with the role of a priest in pagan religious rites, or with the role of a priest in the Old Testament. Paul was simply serving the people as he preached to them as is the meaning of the words he chose to use in the text of Romans 15:16.

For Catholics to use this text to support their sacerdotal applications (water baptism, marriage, Mass, Eucharist, etc.) is a blatant error in exegesis.

Jesus himself said, "I am the way and the truth and the life. No one comes to the Father except through me" (John 14:6). In 1 Timothy 2:5 we find, "For there is one God and one mediator between God and men, the man Christ Jesus, who gave himself as a ransom for all men."

We are told more than once in the New Testament that the death and mediator-ship of Christ was a one-time, once-for-all occurrence. The italicization in the following is by this author for emphasis.

> For Christ died for sins *once for all*, the righteous for the unrighteous, to bring you to God" (1 Peter 3:18).

> He did not enter by means of the blood of goats and calves; but he entered the Most Holy Place *once for all* by his own blood, having obtained eternal redemption (Heb. 9:12).

> So Christ was sacrificed *once* to take away the sins of many people; and he will appear a second time, not to bear sin, but to bring salvation to those who are waiting for him (Heb. 9:28).

> The law is only a shadow of the good things that are coming—not the realities themselves. For this reason, it can never, by the same sacrifices repeated endlessly year after year [or, every time a Catholic Mass is offered as a sacrifice], make perfect those who draw near to worship. If it could, would they not have stopped being offered? For the worshipers would have been cleansed *once for all*, and would no longer have felt guilty for their sins (Heb. 10:1–2).

> And by that will [God's will], we have been made holy through the sacrifice of the body of Jesus Christ *once for all* (Heb. 10:10).

Sacrifices are no longer necessary in any phase of worship; particularly they are not necessary in acts of prayer.

Besides observing from the above texts that our salvation was accomplished in Christ once for all, and only once, notice also that, "we have been made holy." That is, those of us who believe and put our trust in Christ are made holy. That is one reason sacrifices are no longer necessary.

Now, arrayed against the above texts of Scripture and what they teach us about Jesus, salvation, worship, and prayer, we have the phenomenon of popery: mere men who declare themselves to be the infallible, the one and only, and the worldwide representative of Christ—no less than the Vicar of Christ. And, they take upon themselves the sacerdotal role of priest, and furthermore, ordain others as priests.

The popes, by inference, take the Old Testament role of high priest. The bishops and regular Catholic priests are by inference in the role of the Old Testament Levitical priesthood.

That is the basis of the Catholic religious system regarding popes, bishops, and priests. The apostle Paul made this declaration, "Christ is the end of the law so that there may be righteousness for everyone who believes" (Rom. 10:4). The law Paul referred to was the Old Testament law that included the rules governing priests and sacrifices.

The Catholic religious system that is based upon popes, bishops, and priests is defunct. As Paul said, "Christ is the end of [that] law."

The popes claim they are the foundation stone (the rock) upon which all of Christianity is built. They base this on the unmerited claim that Peter was the first pope and each pope in succession inherited from Peter the keys to the kingdom of heaven.

It is their claim that they have the authority (again, the keys) to forgive sins, or to not forgive sins thus sending people to purgatory (eventually to heaven) or to hell.

Who were these men who started this awful heresy? Were they really representatives of Christ? Was there really an unbroken chain of successive popes who had the right to call themselves the Vicars of Christ—who had the authority to send people to purgatory or hell? Today, does Pope Francis, and only Pope Francis, have those keys?

Of course, if you've read the previous chapters, you know none of this is true.

But, who were these popes (priests) who stood between the people and their God? Did they have the authority to ordain other men as priests who then acted as if they possessed the keys to the kingdom? Who and what were these men in reality?

Following are some selected quotes from one era of history that present a disturbing picture of the state of the Roman Catholic religion and its leaders.

Will Durant in his book, *The Reformation,* had the following comments:

> The great dream broke on the nature of man. The administrators of the papal judiciary proved human, biased, venal, even extortionate.[10]

> Throughout the fourteenth century, the Church suffered political humiliation and moral decay. She had begun with the profound sincerity and devotion of Peter and Paul; she had grown into a majestic system of familial, scholastic, social, international discipline, order, and morality; she was now degenerating into a vested interest absorbed in self-perpetuation and finance.[11]

William Durand, Bishop of Mende, submitted to the Council of Vienne (1311) a treatise containing these words:

The whole Church might be reformed if the Church of Rome would begin by removing evil examples from herself . . . by which men are scandalized, and the whole people, as it were, infected. . . . For in all lands . . . the Church of Rome is in ill repute, and all cry and publish it abroad that within her bosom all men, from the greatest even unto the least, have set their hearts upon covetousness. . . . That the whole Christian folk take from the clergy pernicious examples of gluttony is clear and notorious, since the clergy feast more luxuriously . . . than princes and kings.[12]

In 1430 . . . a German envoy to Rome sent his prince a letter that almost sounded the theme and tocsin [warning bell] of the Reformation:

Greed reigns supreme in the Roman court, and day by day finds new devices . . . for extorting money from Germany. . . . Hence much outcry and heartburning. . . . Many questions in regard to the papacy will arise, or else obedience will at last be entirely renounced, to escape from these outrageous exactions by the Italians; and this latter course, as I perceive, would be acceptable to many countries.[13]

The following quote is rather lengthy, but it encompasses much of what was consistently the character of many popes. We can hardly imagine any of these men being Vicars of Christ. The record in the quotes above, and in what follows, simply points out the inherent heresy of the notion that popes were the one and only, worldwide, and infallible representatives of Christ. If that were true, well, I have to say that I wouldn't believe in Christ.

The faults of the papal court mounted as the fifteenth century neared its end. Paul II wore a papal tiara that outweighed a palace in its worth. Sixtus IV made his nephew a millionaire, entered avidly into the game of politics, blessed the cannon that fought his battles, and financed his wars by selling church offices to the highest bidders [which was called simony and was highly discredited]. Innocent VIII celebrated in the Vatican the marriages of his children [he was obviously not celibate]. Alexander VI, like Luther and Calvin, thought clerical celibacy a mistake, and begot five or more children before subsiding into reasonable continence as a pope. His gay virility did not stick so sharply in the gullet of the time as we might suppose; a certain clandestine amorousness was then accepted as usual in the clergy; what offended Europe was that Alexander's unscrupulous diplomacy, and the ruthless generalship of his son Caesar Borgia, rewon the Papal States for the papacy and added needed revenues and strength to the Apostolic See. In these policies and campaigns the Borgias used all those methods of stratagem and death which were soon to be formulated in Machiavelli's *Prince* (1513) as indispensable to founding a powerful state or a united Italy. Pope Julius II out-Caesared Borgia in waging war against rapacious Venice and the invading French; he escaped whenever he could from the prison of the Vatican, led his army in person, and relished the rough life and speech of martial camps. Europe was shocked to see the papacy not only secularized but militarized; . . . It was Julias who began the building of the new St. Peter's, and first granted indulgences to those who contributed to its cost. It was in his pontificate that Luther came to Rome and saw for himself that "sink of iniquity" which had been Lorenzo de' Medici's name for the capital of Christendom.[14]

There is no point in quoting more of the same kinds of material. There is a lot of it.

However, the issue in this chapter concerns the veracity of these men who were designated as popes (Vicars of Christ, representatives of Christ, the one and only representatives, holding the keys of heaven and hell). Were they truly, and as is believed by millions, still the sole authority of Christ on this earth? This question includes, of course, Pope Francis.

Let's look at it this way. The Roman Catholic religion teaches that there is a chain (a succession) of popes (including the bad ones of whom some are mentioned in the quotes above). The chain from Jesus to Peter reaches to and through every pope who has held that office: 295+.

Let's, then, imagine a real chain made up of more than 295 links. What happens to a real chain that is supporting a load if just one of the links breaks? We know what will happen to the load. Can that link be replaced? It would do no good as the load has fallen and is shattered. And, what if a whole section of the chain was faulty: that is, a number of links failed?

And, as we have learned, the very rock the chain is attached to (Peter) is a myth. The chain is attached to thin air.

In the quotes cited previously concerning the various popes, which was not, in truth, a complete list of faulty and immoral popes, and considering that the sordid details of their lives were not completely spelled out either, we can quickly conclude these men did not represent Jesus.

What did they represent? They represented a false religion: the Roman Catholic religion.

So, we must ask, how could anyone trust the eternal state of their souls and spirits to such men and to such a religion? How could anyone trust their eternal future to a religious system that promotes such men and their religious rules, rites, and rituals?

We could make the great mistake that millions have by equating Christianity with Roman Catholicism.

Jesus is, according to the Bible, the only answer to the question of eternal destiny. No man and no religious system can substitute for Jesus. The Holy Spirit is Jesus' only designated representative on this earth. "If you love me, you will obey what I command. And I will ask the Father, and he will give you another Counselor to be with you forever—the Spirit of truth. The world cannot accept him, because it neither sees him nor knows him. But you know him, for he lives with you and will be in you" (John 14:15–17).

Jesus said, "I am the way and the truth and the life. No one comes to the Father except through me" (John 14:6). Jesus backed up his claim by his sinless life, by his miraculous acts of mercy, by pointing to his fulfillment of prophecy from the Old Testament, by his resurrection, and by his ascension into heaven.

Men and women have been trying to get to God by many different means. Even those like many Roman Catholics who claim to be Christians, are trying to get to God through a system of false mediators, rites, and rituals.

Popes, priests, dead Roman Catholics who were labeled *Saints*, and even Mary was brought into play to try to convince God to answer the believing Catholics' prayers. As we will see in a later chapter, even money was used to influence God's will, and to get people through purgatory.

Whatever happened to Jesus and the Holy Spirit?

Because Mary seems to have become the top mediator (the everyday mediator—the Rosary, you know) between God and the Catholic believer, the next chapter is a detailed look at the Mary of the Bible, not the Mary the Roman Catholics have created.

You will see that the Mary of the New Testament was and is not portrayed in any way shape or form as a go-between who arranges for Jesus to hear our prayers. In fact, you will see that Mary was considered nothing more than the temporary mother of Jesus.

P.S. Any reader can easily discover for himself/herself the underbelly of the atrocious, diabolical, anti-Christian acts of leaders of the Roman Catholic religion. Log onto the Internet and write any of these four identifying phrases into the search engine: Spanish Inquisition, Roman Inquisition (these two inquisitions are not the same historical events), the Renaissance popes, and/or the Crusades. The facts of these acts of treachery, torture, murder, and expulsion, which were either instituted by popes or done with the support of popes, will amaze the you.

Humpty Dumpty sat on a wall. Humpty Dumpty had a great fall. All the king's horses and all the king's men couldn't put Humpty Dumpty together again.

The charges (Scriptures) are being packed around the pillars. The implosion is pending.

CHAPTER 6

MARY, THE TEMPORARY MOTHER OF JESUS

OVER MANY YEARS, the Roman Catholic version of Mary has evolved to include her sinless perfection (Immaculate Conception), eternal virginity, assumption into heaven, her mediatorship (mediatrix) with Jesus, and she is considered the "Queen over all things."[1]

Probably, the most significant, blasphemous claim made for Mary is that she is the Mother of God. We must begin here as the refutation of this claim sets the stage for everything else said in this chapter.

Jesus, before he came to earth (the incarnation), has always existed as God. God has no mother. Two passages of Scripture that substantiate Jesus' eternal existence as God are:

> In the beginning was the Word, and the Word was with God, and the Word was God. He was with God in the beginning. Through him all things were made; without him nothing was made that has been made. In him was life, and

that life was the light of men. The light shines in the darkness, but the darkness has not understood it (John 1:1–5).

Who, being in very nature God, did not consider equality with God something to be grasped, but made himself nothing, taking the very nature of a servant, being made in human likeness. And being found in appearance as a man, he humbled himself and became obedient to death—even death on a cross! Therefore, God exalted him to the highest place and gave him the name that is above every name, that at the name of Jesus every knee should bow, in heaven and on earth and under the earth, and every tongue confess that Jesus Christ is Lord, to the glory of God the Father (Phil. 2:6–11).

It is blasphemous to name Mary as the Mother of God. She was the human, temporary, mother of the Son of Man. Jesus, with few exceptions, always referred to himself as the Son of Man. As Paul said in his letter to the Philippians, cited above, Jesus was, "made in human likeness." Mary's role was to be the woman to nurture and to deliver the seed that would become the Son of Man: God in human likeness. Mary was only the human mother of Jesus, the Son of Man. Mary was not the Mother of God.

How could a human being like Mary be the Mother of the eternally existing God?

Roman Catholic leaders have made other claims of Mary over the years. Following are some statements from the 1994 version of the official *Catechism of the Catholic Church*. Between each statement will be this author's comments. "By pronouncing her 'fiat' [an authoritative determination] at the Annunciation [the announcement of the Incarnation] and giving her consent to the Incarnation, Mary was already collaborating with the whole work her Son was to accomplish. She is mother wherever he is Savior and head of the Mystical Body."[2]

It cannot be doubted that in this official dogma it is said, by inference, that Mary had to give her consent to the Incarnation—the birth of Jesus—the coming of the Son of God into this world. It is also said that Mary collaborated with Jesus in all of his work. This implies that Jesus had to have Mary's consent to come to earth and to do what he did. Do you believe this? "The Most Blessed Virgin Mary, when the course of her earthly life was completed, was taken up body and soul into the glory of heaven, where she already shares in the glory of her Son's Resurrection, anticipating the resurrection of all members of his Body."[3]

This statement said, by inference, that Mary didn't experience physical death as all of the rest of mankind does. Do you believe this? What evidence exists to support this claim? To be frank, the evidence of Mary's assumption is just as bereft of proof as that of Mohammed rising into heaven from the Temple Mount on his horse. "We believe that the Holy Mother of God, the new Eve, Mother of the Church, continues in heaven to exercise her maternal role on behalf of the members of Christ."[4]

In this statement, it is implied that Mary is the interceding Mother of all who believe in Christ. In practical terms, as is evidenced by the universal use of the Rosary by most Catholics, Mary confers with Jesus in heaven and helps him to understand the believer's prayers and sees to it that Jesus answers the believer's prayers.

Do you believe that? What scriptural evidence supports this claim? "The Church's devotion to the Blessed Virgin is intrinsic to Christian worship." The Church rightly honors "the Blessed Virgin with special devotion. From the most ancient times the

Blessed Virgin has been honored with the title of 'Mother of God,' to whose protection the faithful fly in all their dangers and needs . . ."[5]

In the above quote, we see Mary as actually receiving devotion. What does that mean? The Catholics will tell you they aren't really worshipping Mary, but notice in the quote that this devotion is "intrinsic to worship." What kind of double-talk is this? Webster's defines devotion as, "an act of prayer or private worship."

In the above four statements, we get the idea of how Catholics view Mary and relate to Mary. We also clearly understand that Mary was not a normal human being if we believe those statements from the official Catholic catechism. To emphasize her non-humanness, Mary K. Doyle in her book, *Grieving with Mary,* said: "She is the only human conceived without the stain of Original Sin—a mark passed on to us as a result of the actions of Adam and Eve. Her Immaculate Conception was told in early Christian hymns and writings by . . . Saint Ambrose and Saint Augustine. Pope Pius X officially proclaimed this truth in the dogma of the Immaculate Conception. . . . December 8, 1854."[6]

To sum up, we are told that:

1. Mary was born sinless.
2. Mary is a virgin in perpetuity. That is, Mary never had other children.
3. Jesus had to confer with her as to when he could come to be born from her womb, and she is involved in all the rest of Jesus' acts including the work of redemption.
4. She was translated into heaven without having to die a physical death.
5. She is the Mother of all believers.

6. She is the Mother of God.
7. She makes sure believers' prayers are heard by Jesus.
8. She is the Queen of heaven.
9. And, as is widely believed by Catholics, she speaks to people on earth at her shrines that are at different geographical locations, which means she is always available anywhere there is a shrine. Some claim to have been healed of illness at these shrines.

Something may be left out in the above list, but we certainly can't fail to get the point that Mary is considered to be by Catholics the most important person in heaven as concerns us mortals.

Now, we must look at what the Bible said about Mary. Is she all of the above and maybe more? Or was the Mary of the Bible just another normal human being who was chosen (with her concurrence; so say Catholic theologians) to bear the seed of Jesus at his incarnation?

We must remember, as we compare and contrast what Catholicism said about Mary, that it wasn't Mary herself, nor Jesus, nor any of his disciples and apostles who said these things; it was the Catholic popes and their advisors.

In other words, we will be comparing and contrasting Scripture with the declarations (dogmas) of the Catholic popes as those dogmas were pronounced over the course of many years, and several popes.

We will begin where the Bible begins, with Matthew's gospel.

This is how the birth of Jesus Christ came about: His mother Mary was pledged to be married to Joseph, but before they came together, she was found to be with child through the Holy Spirit. Because Joseph her husband was a righteous man and did not want to expose her to public disgrace, he had in mind to divorce her quietly.

But after he had considered this, an angel of the Lord appeared to him in a dream and said, "Joseph son of David, do not be afraid to take Mary home as your wife, because what is conceived in her is from the Holy Spirit. She will give birth to a son, and you are to give him the name Jesus, because he will save his people from their sins."

All this took place to fulfill what the Lord had said through the prophet: "The virgin will be with child and will give birth to a son, and they will call him Immanuel"— which means, "God with us."

When Joseph woke up, he did what the angel of the Lord had commanded him and took Mary home as his wife. But he had no union with her until she gave birth to a son. And he gave him the name Jesus (Matt. 1:18–24).

Matthew provides one view of the basic story of the Incarnation—the coming of the Son of God to this earth—the human birth of the Son of Man. Luke, in his gospel, also presents the birth of Jesus but with some different features. We need to read Luke's version, too, but we will bring in that version when it supports something Matthew said or adds something pertinent to this discussion that Matthew didn't say.

Here are some things to note that help us in understanding who Mary was. Keep in mind that we have no other historical record from which to base any judgments about Mary.

Matthew tells us the following about Mary.

1. Mary and Joseph were pledged to marry, which means, in that society, they were virtually considered to be married. The marriage wasn't consummated, but it would be.
2. Before the consummation, Mary became pregnant.

3. The child was "through the Holy Spirit." (Verse 20 says, "what is conceived in her is from the Holy Spirit.")

4. Obviously a miracle occurred as the Holy Spirit placed within Mary's womb the seed that would become the person we know as Jesus. Being a miracle, there is no way we can explain how, in what biological way, this was made to happen.

5. Mary was a virgin in the human sense of that term. She and Joseph had not had intercourse, had not consummated their marriage. Matthew 1: 22 and 23 say, "All this took place to fulfill what the Lord had said through the prophet: 'The virgin will be with child and will give birth to a son, and they will call him Immanuel!'—which means 'God with us.'" If this child, Jesus, had not come from the Holy Spirit, he could not have been titled *Immanuel*—"God with us."

6. Verses 24 and 25 make a further point. "When Joseph woke up, he did what the angel of the Lord had commanded him and took Mary home as his wife. But he had no union with her until she gave birth to a son." This is very important. Note, it says, "he had no union [intercourse] with her *until* she gave birth to a son." The word *until* is italicized by this author for emphasis.

7. The obvious meaning of the word *until* is that they did have intercourse afterward. Remember the principle of interpretation mentioned in the Introduction of this book: When the Scriptures make plain sense, seek no other sense. It makes plain sense that Joseph and Mary would consummate their marriage in the normal way of a man and wife and the word *until* means that they did exactly that.

8. We have at least three instances in the Scriptures that affirm Joseph and Mary had children. Some men in the synagogue in his home town of Nazareth (Mark 6:3) exclaimed, "Isn't this Mary's son and the brother of James, Joseph, Judas and Simon? Aren't his sisters here with us?" What could be more clear? That Jesus had brothers is also mentioned in Mark 3:31 when Mary brought Jesus' brothers with her to rescue Jesus: "Then Jesus' mother and brothers arrived. Standing outside, they sent someone in to call him. A crowd was sitting around him, and they told him, 'Your mother and brothers are outside looking for you.'" In Acts 1:14 it is said: "They all joined together constantly in prayer, along with the women and Mary the mother of Jesus, and with his brothers." Jesus had four brothers and at least two sisters. In Mark 6:3, the word *sisters* is plural.

9. Was Mary a perpetual virgin; obviously not. On what basis, then, do the Roman Catholics declare her to be a perpetual virgin?

Catholics also declare that Mary was born without sin (Immaculate Conception). In Luke's Gospel, Mary is credited with speaking these words (called the Magnificat): "And Mary said: 'My soul glorifies the Lord and my spirit rejoices in God my Savior'" (Luke 1:46–47). Note that Mary addressed the Lord as, "God, my Savior."

Plain sense makes it clear that Mary recognized her need for a Savior. This is a tacit admission on her part that she was just like the rest of us, a sinner. Is there any other way this can be interpreted? It's clear, and it's from her own mouth.

So, we must conclude there was no such thing, regarding Mary, as an Immaculate Conception. Mary isn't the Mother of God, she wasn't a perpetual virgin, and she wasn't without sin.

It is also claimed that Mary is the key to answered prayers because, being the mother of Jesus, she has his ear. As one twelve-year-old girl (the granddaughter of a friend), raised under the influence of Catholicism, said, "I pray to Mary because God and Jesus are too busy taking care of the world." Where did she get that idea?

Doyle put it this way: "Our prayers do not end with Mary but continue through her. We are asking her to pray our intentions and take them to her son."[7] Doyle also made this statement showing that some Catholics rely on Mary for more than mere mediation: "Wearing a scapular is the mark of a pledge of allegiance to Mary. With its use, we are asking our Holy Mother for her constant protection and assistance. Our Lady promised St. Simon Stock on July 16, 1251, that while wearing it the wearer thinks of her and, therefore, she thinks of the wearer. She also said that those who die while wearing a scapular will not suffer the fires of hell, because the devil is powerless in its [the scapular's] presence."[8]

A scapular is (there are slightly different designs) basically a band of cloth with an opening for the head that is worn over the shoulders. Note the superstitious nature of Doyle's explanation. Wearing this garment supposedly provides Mary's "constant protection and assistance." And if you are wearing it when you die, you won't go to hell.

How many Catholics have you seen going down the street with a scapular on their shoulders? Actually, it seems the only Catholics authorized to wear a scapular are priests and nuns.

What is this all about? It is just another example of the superstitious and mythological nature of Marian doctrines. Many more of these kinds of superstitious beliefs could be cited. Superstition, according to Webster's is, "A belief or practice resulting from ignorance, fear of the unknown, trust in magic or chance, or a false conception of causation." Reading Doyle's book, or reading any number of other books about the rituals of Catholicism will provide all the examples necessary to prove the true nature of Marianism (the collection of dogmas associated with Mary as described at the beginning of this chapter) and the nature of many other Catholic practices where sheer superstition is involved.

We've now examined the Scriptures and some of the doctrines of Catholicism regarding the birth of Jesus.

It's time to look into the Scriptures, the only actual historical source available, and view Mary in her life and actions as portrayed in the Bible. We need to see the real Mary.

The reader might be surprised at how Mary is portrayed in the Scriptures, at least by this author's interpretations of her actions. Mary is not an enigma, just a normal human mother with an abnormal responsibility and relationship to Jesus.

We know that Mary and Joseph were very sensitive to the Lord God and lived by the requirements of the law (the law of Moses, as it was called). We will follow the story as told by Luke.

Parenthetically, it is interesting to ask where was Joseph in all of this? A couple of things can be noted. After the birth of Jesus, when Joseph and Mary were instructed to flee Bethlehem, go to Egypt, later return, and go back to Nazareth, the angel's directions were always given to Joseph, not to Mary.

Also, we must realize that Joseph was in on giving birth to, and raising, at least seven children; one of those being Jesus; Jesus would have been the half-brother, in human terms, of the others. Even though Joseph seems to disappear from the biblical record, he was obviously on the scene for a number of years.

Leaving the parenthetical, the following presentation sections of Luke's Gospel will be quoted with a following commentary by this author. "In the sixth month [of Elizabeth's pregnancy with John the Baptist], God sent the angel Gabriel to Nazareth, a town in Galilee, to a virgin pledged to be married to a man named Joseph, a descendant of David. The virgin's name was Mary. The angel went to her and said, 'Greetings, you who are highly favored! The Lord is with you'" (Luke 1:26–28).

In the Latin Vulgate translation of the Bible, the words *highly favored* were translated: "full of grace." The Roman Catholics erroneously interpreted this to mean:

> The blessed Virgin's fullness of grace made her of all creatures the nearest to the Author of grace. . . . Mary's initial grace surpassed even the final grace of the angels and of all other saints. . . . Hence, according to tradition, Mary's merits and prayer, could, even without any angel or saint, obtain even here on earth more than could all saints and angels without her. . . . From her divine maternity and her fullness of grace, arises Mary's function of universal mediatrix, a title given to her by tradition, and now consecrated by a feast of the Church universal . . . by interceding she obtains and distributes all graces which we receive . . . which has given her the title of coredemptrix, in the sense that with, by, and in Christ she redeemed the human race.[9]

From the phrase, *full of grace* (which isn't even a correct translation), Catholicism said, "according to tradition (not the Scriptures)," Mary is the source of all grace for everyone else, she is the universal mediator between God and all mankind, and she helped redeem the human race.

That is quite an accomplishment rising out of three words—full of grace—which words aren't the original—in the Greek language—of what was said. The meaning of the Greek words was, "you who are highly favored."

Moving on in chapter 1 of Luke's gospel: "At that time Mary got ready and hurried to a town in the hill country of Judea, where she entered Zechariah's home and greeted Elizabeth" (Luke 1:39–40).

It seems as if Mary, without telling Joseph, whom she was pledged to marry, got on a donkey (assuming this was her mode of travel) and headed for Elizabeth's home. She stayed with Elizabeth for about three months and returned to Nazareth.

It also seems clear, taking the biblical narrative just as it stands and comparing the two narratives (Matthew and Luke), that Mary took off for Elizabeth's without telling Joseph. She may have told him, but based upon her subsequent actions (or lack of action toward Joseph) it is possible she didn't tell Joseph she was leaving. If so, she was gone three months, and Joseph knew nothing of her whereabouts or the angel's visit to Mary or that Mary was pregnant.

When she returns from Elizabeth's, she is three months pregnant. It is at this time that Joseph becomes aware Mary is pregnant. As we shall see, Joseph is later visited by an angel who explains what has happened.

But, at the moment Joseph meets Mary, I can hear Joseph saying to her, "Where have you been? You've gained some weight." At this point, Mary might have answered, "I've been visiting Elizabeth, and I'm pregnant."

Obviously, she still hasn't told Joseph the whole story about the angel's visit and that she was carrying the Messiah in her womb.

Joseph, without knowing the facts, became so upset when he found out Mary was pregnant that he considered a divorce. That's when the angel stepped in and told Joseph, in a dream, why and how Mary got pregnant.

What does this scenario tell us about Mary? I will leave that for you to decide, but Mary's lack of communication with Joseph could be interpreted in a way that would throw a negative light on Mary.

The angel didn't tell Mary to keep all of this secret and hidden from Joseph. She apparently never intended to tell Joseph, as we see the angel stepping in to fill in this gap in poor communication between this espoused couple. Maybe Mary was afraid to tell Joseph. Maybe she thought Joseph wouldn't believe her, but all in all, it was a strange way for Mary to act. I admit this is reading between the lines. But, what do you think?

We see Mary in action again at the time Jesus turned the water into wine. "On the third day, a wedding took place at Cana in Galilee. Jesus' mother was there, and Jesus and his disciples had also been invited to the wedding. When the wine was gone, Jesus' mother said to him, 'They have no more wine.' 'Dear woman, why do you involve me?' Jesus replied, 'My time has not yet come.' His mother said to the servants, 'Do whatever he tells you'" (John 2:1–5).

What an interesting exchange between Jesus and Mary. I don't think Mary knew exactly what Jesus would do, but she knew he would be able to solve this problem. Jesus made it clear to Mary that he didn't want to solve the problem. Jesus asked Mary a question, "Dear woman, why do you involve me?" Then Jesus stated to Mary, "My time has not yet come."

Notice that Mary plowed right through Jesus' reluctance and said to the servants, "Do whatever he tells you." Now isn't that interesting! Did Mary want a miracle for her own self-satisfaction? Did she want the prestige of being the mother of the miracle man? I'm inferring the possibility of some spurious motives on Mary's part. I want the reader to seriously consider who this woman was—was she a sinless goddess or a normal mother and a sinner like you and me?

It is notable that in this exchange, Jesus addresses Mary as "Dear woman." He doesn't say, "Oh, come on Mom." What has Jesus done here by addressing Mary as woman? There is no doubt Jesus had no intention to be derogatory.

However, it appears he was intending to put distance between himself and Mary. He was sending her a signal which she entirely missed as is evident from another incident, as we shall see, from Mark's gospel.

There is some background to the incident in Mark's gospel, chapter 3, that is necessary for us to have in view. Jesus had been preaching in the synagogue. During these moments, Jesus healed a man with a shriveled hand. "Another time he went into the synagogue, and a man with a shriveled hand was there. Some of them [Pharisees] were looking for a reason to accuse Jesus, so they watched him closely to see if he would heal him on the Sabbath. . . . Then the Pharisees went out and began to plot with the Herodians how they might kill Jesus" (Mark 3:1–6).

The plot to kill Jesus was simmering in the background as Jesus moved on and continued healing people. The story progresses in chapter 3 to the point that the crowds were being stirred up by the Scribes (Jewish religious lawyers) who were sent from Jerusalem for that very purpose. The Scribes accused Jesus of being from Satan and healing people by the power of Satan.

The situation was getting heated. Apparently, the crowd was beginning to respond to the accusations of the Scribes. Jesus' family was now hearing about what was going on and particularly the threat to Jesus' life. "When his family heard about this, they went to take charge of him, for they said, 'He is out of his mind'" (Mark 3:20–21).

No doubt Mary and Jesus' brothers sat around the living room and concocted a plan to rescue Jesus from the mob that was being stimulated by the Pharisees and Scribes, and what a plan.

They were going to announce that Jesus was crazy.

And now Jesus' mother and brothers actually arrived on the scene. The action has shifted from the synagogue to someone's home. "Then Jesus' mother and brothers arrived [note the presence of brothers]. Standing outside, they sent someone in to call him. A crowd was sitting around him, and they told him, 'Your mother and brothers are outside looking for you.' 'Who are my mother and my brothers?' he asked. Then he looked at those seated in a circle around him and said, 'Here are my mother and my brothers! Whoever does God's will is my brother and sister and mother'" (Mark 3:31–35).

Again, we see Jesus putting distance between himself and his entire earthly family, including his mother. We also see Mary organizing a rescue party and trying, as any overprotective mother might do, to deliver Jesus from the mob.

Jesus was having none of it. The family was put in their place, including Mary.

Mary, the mother of Jesus, portrayed to us in the Gospels, seems to have had no real understanding of Jesus in terms of his mission on earth and his destiny. Jesus had to distance himself from her because she was a normal, protective mother and seemed to have some personality traits that got in the way of Jesus as he carried out his earthly commission from God the Father. Even the depth of her belief in Jesus as the Son of God—and God—must come into question.

Could Mary have said to Jesus what Doubting Thomas said, "My Lord and my God?" (John 20:28).

Would Mary have said to Jesus what Peter said, "You are the Christ, the Son of the living God?" (Matt. 16:16).

Those are questions we cannot answer, but doubt is raised when we consider how Mary related to Jesus at the beginning of his adult ministry and during the tenure of his ministry. Doubt is raised when we read of Jesus' need to distance himself from Mary. She seemed not to understand who he really was and what he was about.

There is serious doubt that any other human mother of Jesus would have acted any differently, but that's just the point; Mary was just a human mother, nothing more. Well, she was something more. She was chosen by God the Father, God the Son, and God the Holy Spirit to be the temporary mother of the Son of Man. She would be, in the annals of mankind, blessed.

As we view Mary from the Scriptures, we also observe some other interesting facts about her life.

When Jesus was hanging on the cross, he appointed John to be Mary's son. "Near the cross of Jesus stood his mother. . . . When Jesus saw his mother there, and the disciple whom he loved standing nearby, he said to his mother, 'Dear woman, here is your son,' and to the disciple, 'Here is your mother.' From that time on, this disciple took her into his home" (John 19:25–27).

Once again, we note that Jesus addressed his mother as "woman." Even at this point in his life he had to enforce the separation and distance from his earthly temporary mother.

This was Jesus' last act and his last words with regards to Mary. Why did he do this now? Mary had four natural sons; why John? It seems that Jesus was being emphatic here. Not only was he distancing himself from Mary, but, in a sense, he was denying his relationship to his earthly brothers. At this time, as far as we know, none of Jesus' earthly brothers believed in Jesus. Perhaps what Jesus is pointing to is that Mary and John had a spiritual kinship; John was definitely a disciple, and Mary was coming to that realization for herself. We will see the consummation of Mary's commitment later in this chapter of this book.

Now we must also observe that John later wrote one of the four Gospels, three short letters known as 1, 2, and 3 John, and the book of Revelation. What we need to notice is that John does not mention Mary in any of his writings. Doesn't that seem strange?

If Mary was all of the things the Roman Catholics said she was, wouldn't John have spent a good deal of time in his writings promoting Mary? If anyone was to promote Mary, it would naturally have been John.

The fact is not one other author of any New Testament document promotes Mary or even mentions her. The exception, of course, is the four Gospels, plus one reference in the book of Acts which will be discussed later.

In the book of Galatians, the Apostle Paul says this: "But when the time had fully come, God sent his Son, born of a woman, born under law, to redeem those under law, that we might receive the full rights of sons" (Gal. 4:4).

Paul doesn't even mention who the woman was. It seems the identity of the woman, in Paul's mind, was irrelevant. Wouldn't this have been a great opportunity for this great apostle to have promoted Mary if she were to be promoted as a virtual goddess as is done in Catholicism?

The silence of every post-gospel New Testament author is deafening!

Jesus appeared to his disciples (John 20:19–23), and Mary was not invited. Isn't that interesting in light of what Catholicism says about Mary.

When Paul lists the people who saw Jesus after his resurrection (1 Cor. 15:3–8), he names several but says nothing of Mary being one of them. In other words, Jesus didn't bother to appear to Mary after his resurrection. Doesn't that seem strange if Mary was going to be all that Catholicism claimed for her?

It is even more striking to note that in Paul's comments about those who saw Jesus after the resurrection, he states that Jesus appeared to James, the half-brother of Jesus: "Then he appeared to James, then to all the apostles" (1 Cor. 15:7). The text notes in the NIV translation make it clear this James was the half-brother of Jesus. It was, apparently, when Jesus appeared to James that James first believed who Jesus was.

What is striking is that Jesus appeared to James and not to Mary. James was to become a leader of the church in Jerusalem. Mary disappears from the pages of the Bible.

There is a passage of Scripture in the book of Hebrews that is most interesting as we consider the role of Mary in Jesus' life. In Hebrews 6:20(b) it is said of Jesus, "He has become a high priest forever, in the order of Melchizedek."

After mentioning some other characteristics of Melchizedek, in Hebrews 7:3, this statement is made: "Without father or mother, without genealogy, without beginning of days or end of life, like the Son of God he remains a priest forever."

It is obvious the writer of Hebrews, in context, is speaking of Jesus when he says, "without father or mother." What could this mean in terms of Mary as the human mother of Jesus? Does this have any bearing on the statement that Jesus' conception was, "of the Holy Spirit"?

The last mention of Mary in the Scriptures is: "They all [waiting for the promised Holy Spirit] joined together constantly in prayer, along with the women and Mary the mother of Jesus, and with his brothers" (Acts 1:14).

Do we once again hear an echo of John the Baptist's statement, "He must become greater; I must become less"? (John 3:30).

That was John the Baptist's testimony, and we note that Joseph, Jesus' temporary father, also disappeared from the historical record. And after Acts 1:14, there is no further mention of Mary in any other Scripture.

Mary, no doubt, would echo the Baptist's testimony if she had been given the chance: "He must become greater; I must become less." Perhaps that is what was going through her mind that day at the cross when Jesus put her under John's care. Or, maybe John the Baptist's words were in her mind as she and Jesus' brothers joined the prayer meeting while waiting for the Holy Spirit.

There are, of course, certain things we cannot know. However, it is very dangerous for anyone to teach as truth what is merely imaginary.

As we reviewed the dogmas of the Catholic religion regarding Mary at the beginning of this chapter, and now as we've looked at the Mary of the Bible, it can only be concluded that the Roman Catholic theologians (popes, bishops, priests, etc.)

used their own imaginations and thoughts to develop the traditions, legends, and myths that they teach about Mary.

As has been shown in this chapter, there is no scriptural basis for any (not one) of the promoted Catholic beliefs about Mary.

Anytime anyone promotes any doctrines, or dogmas, that are outside of the words, principles, promises, and patterns put down in Scripture, they are going to come under judgment sooner or later.

God said to the children of Israel through Moses, "See that you do all I command you; do not add to it or take away from it" (Deut. 12:32). This same admonition is part of the last words of the book of Revelation: "I warn everyone who hears the words of the prophecy of this book: If anyone adds anything to them, God will add to him the plagues described in this book. And if anyone takes words away from this book of prophecy, God will take away from him his share in the tree of life and in the holy city, which are described in this book" (Rev. 22:18–19).

Those two admonitions from the Old and New Testaments both specify not to add or take away anything from God's Word. The judgments are of two categories: plagues and loss of eternal life in the holy city.

Peter said: "But there were also false prophets among the people, just as there will be false teachers among you. They will secretly introduce destructive heresies even denying the sovereign Lord who bought them—bringing swift destruction on themselves. Many will follow their shameful ways and will bring the way of truth into disrepute. In their greed these teachers will exploit you with stories they have made up. Their condemnation has long been hanging over them, and their destruction has not been sleeping" (2 Peter 2:1–3).

And what was the fundamental method of the false teachers: "stories they have made up." As Peter also said, "We did not follow cleverly invented stories when we told you about the power and coming of our Lord Jesus Christ, but we were eyewitnesses of his majesty" (2 Peter 1:16).

"Cleverly invented stories" are not the hallmark of the authors of the Bible.

If there is any Roman Catholic reading this, I hope you are seriously considering what you believe about Catholicism, and specifically, from this chapter, what you believe about Mary.

I have deliberately tried to shock the reader, if he or she needs to be shocked, by my depiction of Mary as a normal human being, wife and mother; a sinner in need of a Savior.

Scriptural charges are being set around the pillars of Catholicism; the grand implosion is pending.

But, surely, the reader must already be aware and convinced that these three important pillars of the Catholic religious system (Peter, the popes, and Mary) are actually fabrications constructed, if you will, solely of sand.

The next chapter begins the discussion of the sacramental system devised by Catholic leaders. The sacramental system has four pillars that serve as, in my judgment, the foundational doctrines necessary to bring each Catholic believer under the control of the local and universal Catholic hierarchy. Control, is after all, the essential fact and necessity of this religious system. All religious cults share this motivation.

The next chapter is an introduction to the sacramental system of Catholic religion, and the fundamental doctrinal pillar of that system: Tradition.

It is the doctrine of Tradition that sets up, establishes, and enables all the other erroneous doctrines, which together constitute the sacramental system of Catholicism.

Just to remind the reader: Peter, the popes, and Mary have been identified as the three people pillars of the system, and Tradition, now the fourth pillar, will be added as one of the seven pillars.

From this point on, we will be discussing certain dogmas, not people, and it is these dogmas that complete the faulty structure upon which Catholic leaders have built their system.

CHAPTER 7

TRADITION TRUMPS SCRIPTURE

DEAR READER, YOU have just witnessed through the first chapters of this book that the Roman Catholic religion has no legitimate foundation; a foundation that was based upon the illegitimate claim Peter was a bishop of Rome and the first pope.

In fact, Nicolas Cheetham, one of their own historians wrote when referring to Peter, "The lack of any concrete evidence of the later stage of his [Peter's] life and his relationship with Paul at the time of the latter's residence at Rome is very puzzling. Many scholars, from Marilius of Padua (1326) onwards, have questioned whether he was in Rome at all. . . . If it was just a legend, along with the story of his martyrdom, the origin and meaning of the papacy would of course be invalidated." [1]

Of course, the whole history is a fabrication. That fabrication was amply demonstrated in chapters 2 through 5 by circumstantial and biblical evidence. Peter was certainly not the first pope and was likely never in Rome.

Therefore, we must conclude the entire Roman Catholic religious system is without merit—is invalidated as Cheetham admits.

Adding to the Peter/pope historical debacle, it was also clear from biblical evidence Peter was not the rock upon which Jesus the Christ would build his church, and that Peter did not hold the keys to the kingdom solely and in perpetuity.

Thus, there is no such thing as apostolic succession with subsequent popes up to and including the current pope who also, then, would hold the keys to the kingdom of heaven.

The foundations of Roman Catholicism were clearly not biblical and were fabrications engineered by the back-filling of history, which is admitted by honest historians.

In the process of building the Catholic system, Mary became another pillar of their religion. Biblical evidence reveals the true Mary of gospel history, her relationship to Jesus, and her being dropped out of the biblical narrative. The Marian doctrines perpetrated by Roman Catholics are so disingenuous and so without biblical merit one can scarcely imagine this hoax was ever believed in the first place.

When Cheetham said, "the meaning of the papacy would of course be invalidated," he also said, "What surely matters is the strength of the tradition handed down from the early days of Christianity in Rome." He further stated, "It is irrelevant that the tradition later became encrusted with legend."[2]

What was this tradition he wrote about? How can tradition and legend be irrelevant?

At this point, we will examine one of the fundamental errors of Roman Catholic religious leaders. It was this error that led to much of Roman Catholic heresy. It is this error that leads to other errors that will be examined in the following chapters.

In *The Counter-Reformation*, B. J. Kidd devotes a long chapter to what in history is known as the Council of Trent. The Council of Trent was put in motion by Pope Paul III in May 1542. However, the Council did not actually convene until December 1545. It was to meet in three different sessions over the course of eighteen years, beginning in 1545 and ending in 1563.[3] The decisions of this Council are often referred to in history books as Tridentine.

First, a word about the Counter-Reformation. As you may already know, Martin Luther is credited with inaugurating the Protestant Reformation. Actually, there were several men, among them John Wycliffe and John Hus, who preceded Luther with direct actions and teachings that refuted some of the basic beliefs of Catholicism. But it was Luther who startled the Catholic world and subsequently much of Europe with his rebuttal of the use of indulgences to raise money to build St. Peter's Cathedral in Rome.

Generally, an indulgence is offered by popes to anyone who would buy the indulgence with a gift of money or some other asset. The indulgence, then, is issued, which often consists of reduction of time in purgatory the after-death passage that Catholics believe they have to go through to get to heaven. Purgatory is where the Catholic believer is punished for his/her sins and, in a sense, cleaned up so they will be fit for heaven. The Catholic's time in purgatory could be shortened, even cancelled, depending upon the importance of what the pope wants to accomplish. There will be more about this religious Ponzi scheme in a later chapter.

As Luther delivered lectures and wrote commentaries (particularly on the books of Romans and Galatians), a fundamental issue became starkly clear: the issue of whether the Bible was the sole authority for Christian belief and practice or whether religious leaders could ignore the Bible, add to the Bible, or even contradict the Bible with their own teachings—meaning tradition, legends, and myths.

There were many people who professed to be Christians and who had been Catholics (including several of Luther's peers among the clergy and various European Catholic political leaders) who saw the truth of what Luther was saying: the Scriptures were the only source of belief and practice.

The Protestant Reformation, with Luther as the spearhead, caused the issue of Scripture versus tradition to be a major dividing point between Catholics and Protestants. Literally, thousands of people left the Catholic fold over this issue. In fact, whole countries abandoned Rome and her popes.

Catholic leaders realized they needed to do something to stop this fallout. The Council of Trent was one of the tools the popes used to define their beliefs and get agreement from bishops and priests resident in countries other than Italy.

Kidd, in his book, *The Counter-Reformation*, demonstrates how the Council of Trent was a major move on the part of the Catholic leadership to counter (as in Counter-Reformation) the teachings of the Protestants and secure their position as Vicars of Christ and leaders of the whole Christian world.[4]

The practice of ignoring, adding to, and/or contradicting the Bible had come to be referred to as Tradition; that is, the teachings of Catholic leaders based upon ideas not found in the Bible.

One of the major teachings coming out of the Protestant Reformation was stated in two simple words: *solo scriptura*. This meant the Bible was the only source of truth for the Christian. This became, then, a serious challenge to and in direct opposition to what the Roman Catholics taught, which was that their traditions were a viable source of Christian belief.

The Council of Trent was the official historical meeting at which the concept of Tradition was affirmed and was the major decision opening the door to affirm all of the other heresies perpetrated by Roman Catholics in their religious system. Some of those heresies will be brought to the reader's attention in later chapters.

Consequently, when the Council of Trent finally convened, one of the first issues that had to be dealt with was the issue of Scripture versus Tradition. The Council, "proceeded, in the fourth Session, 8 April 1546, to deal with the important question of the sources of religious truth. They were defined as Scripture and Tradition; and it was laid down that these are of equal authority."[5]

Also, "It was for the Church [meaning the Roman Catholic Church leaders] alone to expound Scripture. And no books of Scripture were to be printed or published without the editor's name and the consent of the Ordinary."[6] The Ordinary was the ordained Roman Catholic bishops. But, in practice, any decisions of this nature would be finally decided in Rome.

"Of these decisions, the first, on the equal authority of Scripture and Tradition, was the most important. Its effect on the subsequent relations of Catholicism and Protestantism was decisive. It rendered reconciliation with the Protestants impossible."[7]

One Cardinal (Cardinal Pole) expressed to the Council how important this issue was to the foundation, development, and maintenance of the Roman Catholic system:

> "These prelates," he replied [prelates, in this case, were voting members of the Council who didn't think that Scripture versus Tradition was a serious matter] "seem scarcely to

understand the importance of the matter in hand. If they would only reflect how our religion as a whole is called in question, they would see that we were not spending time over nothing in urging the reception of Scripture and Tradition as well. The matter, indeed, is of such moment that nothing more serious could engage our attention. . . . Our beliefs, and our worship, in their entirety, depend upon Tradition."[8]

Kidd makes this additional observation concerning the importance of Tradition to the Roman Catholic religious system: "He [Pole] saw too that all subsequent decisions of the Council must follow inevitably from the acceptance of this decree."[9]

That statement by Pole couldn't be more significant. Because when he said, "subsequent decisions of the Council," he meant in essence, and as we shall see later, those subsequent decisions were all of the heresies that would spring forth from this fundamental heresy: Tradition equals Scripture.

One other important idea about the rule of Tradition in the Roman Catholic religious system must be mentioned. In a note at the bottom of page 60, Kidd added this revealing statement from Pope Pius IV when he commented on how Tradition related to Scripture, he said, "the tradition which governs the interpretation of Scripture."[10]

Taking the Pope's statement at face value, one can easily discern that Tradition could even determine the meaning of a particular Scripture passage. In other words, a pope's or bishop's particular bias (Tradition) could rule over how a Scripture passage would be interpreted. If this were the case, Tradition could rule over Scripture. So, it is not just a matter of Scripture and Tradition being equal, but Tradition might supersede Scripture.

As we will see in the coming chapters of this book, that, in fact, is the case with many fundamental Catholic doctrines.

In chapters 2 through 6 of this book, the three pillars of the Roman Catholic religion were revealed for what they are, myths, hoaxes, and heresies. Perhaps you heard and felt the crash as the foundations imploded.

And, there was a superstructure built upon these crumbled foundations. As Cardinal Pole said, "Our beliefs, and our worship, in their entirety, depend upon Tradition." Note: Pole does not say these beliefs and our worship rest upon Scripture, but upon Tradition; and in their entirety.

The Council of Trent was a kind of historical watershed from which flowed official sanction for every significant dogma and decree that would bind every Roman Catholic to laws just as rigid and meaningless as the religious laws binding all others of the world's religions.

These were not new religious laws. These were the dogma and decrees practiced by Roman Catholics for hundreds of years. It wasn't that these religious laws had not been contested over those years; even the primacy of the pope was constantly under attack from some quarters.

Many popes, bishops, and priests failed to support and practice all the dogmas. All of the histories point that out. But as a result of Trent, a house cleaning began which was supported by a rising educational system that brought order, obedience, and security to adherents of the Catholic religious system.

In the chapters following, we will see just how Tradition trumped Scripture as Catholic leaders at the Council of Trent affirmed and fixed their rules, rites, and rituals.

But, before we get to the heresies that spun off of the Tradition issue, it will be good to look into the official twenty-first century catechism of the Catholic religion.

In 1992, Pope John Paul II dedicated an eight-hundred-page document titled, *Catechism of the Catholic Church*. A catechism contains the approved teachings of the religious system it represents.

This catechism was published in English in 1994. Following are some excerpts from the introduction written by Pope John Paul II. "The *Catechism of the Catholic Church* is the result of very extensive collaboration; it was prepared over six years of intense work done in a spirit of complete openness and fervent zeal. In 1986, I entrusted a commission of twelve Cardinals and Bishops, chaired by Cardinal Joseph Ratzinger, with the task of preparing a draft of the catechism requested by the Synod Fathers. An editorial committee of seven diocesan Bishops, experts in theology and catechesis, assisted the commission in its work."[11]

You can tell from reading the above that this catechism is the official statement of the dogmas and doctrines of the Roman Catholic religion.

John Paul adds to the sense of authority of the catechism by the following declarations. "The *Catechism of the Catholic Church*, which I approved June 25th last and the publication of which I today order by virtue of my Apostolic Authority, is a statement of the Church's faith and catholic doctrine, attested to or illumined by Sacred Scripture, the Apostolic Tradition, and the Church's Magisterium. The approval and publication of the *Catechism of the Catholic Church* represent a service which the Successor of Peter wishes to offer to the Holy Catholic Church, to all the particular Churches in peace and communion with the Apostolic See."[12]

The pope further establishes his authority and the authenticity of this document by praying to the Virgin Mary. "At the conclusion of this document presenting the *Catechism of the*

Catholic Church, I beseech the Blessed Virgin Mary, Mother of the Incarnate Word and Mother of the Church, to support with her powerful intercession the catechetical work of the entire Church on every level, at this time when she is called to a new effort of evangelization."[13]

The 1994 *Catechism* was published thirty years after the Second Vatican Council. It must be concluded, then, that any changes in the Catholic religious system coming as a result of that Council, or any other Councils, Synods, etc. up to 1994, were included in this catechism. As far as I know, there has been no other official catechism.

Time and space was taken here to introduce (even though it was previously quoted in the chapter regarding Mary) the Catholic's catechism to you as it will be cited many times in the next chapters. It will be cited along with Scripture to show the discrepancies and contradictions between it and the Scriptures.

You no doubt noticed that Pope John Paul was explicit in telling what the authority of this text and his role in authorizing it were based upon; that was his Apostolic Authority as the Successor of Peter, Sacred Scripture and the Church's Magisterium. Of course, he drew the Virgin Mary into the picture to make sure he had all his ducks in a row, so to speak.

Did you know that Mary was instrumental in evangelism?

You might wonder what he means by the Church's Magisterium? That is just a not-so-subtle way of describing and solidifying the notion of the popes and bishops being the only authorized interpreters and communicators of truth. The word *Magisterium* is built upon the word *majesty.* It speaks of the highest authority: an authority to whom you must submit. Even the Scriptures were required to submit to the interpretation of the Magisterium.

See if you can discern the subtle wording in the following statements regarding the Magisterium and Scripture, and Tradition.

> As a result [of the popes being the successors of the apostles], the Church [meaning the Catholic Church] to whom the transmission and interpretation of Revelation is entrusted, "does not derive her certainty about all revealed truths from the holy Scriptures alone. Both Scripture and Tradition must be accepted and honored with equal sentiments of devotion and reverence.[14]
>
> Yet this Magisterium is not superior to the Word of God, but is its servant. It teaches only what has been handed on to it. At the divine command and with the help of the Holy Spirit, it listens to this devotedly, guards it with dedication, and expounds it faithfully. All that it proposes for belief as being divinely revealed is drawn from this single deposit of faith.[15]

The second paragraph above says, "All that it [the Magisterium] proposes for belief as being divinely revealed is drawn from this single deposit of faith."

But, in the first paragraph quoted above, it says, "Tradition must be accepted and honored with equal sentiments of devotion and reverence."

There was a single deposit of faith: it was the Scriptures. However, in a very subtle word game, Pope John Paul declares that the single deposit of faith is both the Scriptures and Catholic Tradition. As was claimed in the first paragraph, "Tradition must be accepted and honored with equal sentiments of devotion and reverence."

The word *equal* means just that, equal. The Catholic Magisterium believed and based their doctrines upon Scripture and

Tradition. As was previously said, and will be shown later, Tradition actually overruled Scripture in many cases.

One more quote from these same pages will reveal just what they really believed and how interpretation of the Word of God (the Bible, the Scriptures) was intertwined with Tradition. "'The task of giving an authentic interpretation of the Word of God, whether in its written form or in the form of Tradition, has been entrusted to the living, teaching office of the Church alone. Its authority in this matter is exercised in the name of Jesus Christ.' This means that the task of interpretation has been entrusted to the bishops in communion with the successor of Peter [the Magisterium], the Bishop of Rome [the pope]."[16]

Notice in the first sentence of the above quote these words: "The task of giving an authentic interpretation of the Word of God, whether in its written form [the Scriptures] or in the form of Tradition" reveals that they deemed their oral traditions were also the Word of God. One can only wonder at the brazenness of such assertions.

It is important to observe that the Catholics believed interpretation of the Scriptures was "entrusted to the living, teaching office of the Church alone."

Notice, too, that the right to make such an outlandish claim (the Catholic Church alone) rests upon the final authority of the successor of Peter. We already know there was no successor of Peter in terms of apostolic succession that emanated into the Bishop of Rome and that morphed into a pope being the Vicar of Christ.

When one starts out with a lie, the only way to maintain the lie is to keep on lying.

As we examine the lie in more detail in future chapters, it would be good to remind ourselves of the source of such deceit and false doctrines.

In the fifteenth chapter of Matthew's gospel, Jesus has an encounter with some Pharisees and teachers of the law (scribes). Following is an account of that exchange.

> Then some Pharisees and teachers of the law came to Jesus from Jerusalem and asked, "Why do your disciples break the tradition of the elders? They don't wash their hands before they eat!"
>
> Jesus replied, "And why do you break the command of God for the sake of your tradition? For God said, 'Honor your father and mother' and 'Anyone who curses his father or mother must be put to death.' But you say that if a man says to his father or mother, 'Whatever help you might otherwise have received from me is a gift devoted to God,' he is not to 'honor his father' with it. Thus you nullify the word of God for the sake of your tradition. You hypocrites! Isaiah was right when he prophesied about you:
>
> "These people honor me with their lips, but their hearts are far from me. They worship me in vain; their teachings are but rules taught by men" (Matt 15: 1–9).

In the above passage, traditions are identified as rules taught by men. Jesus called such men who teach traditions hypocrites. And he said, "They worship me in vain."

To equate men's religious traditions with Scripture, or to "nullify the word of God for the sake of your tradition," has the most serious ramifications.

Beware! "Not everyone who says to me, 'Lord, Lord,' will enter the kingdom of heaven, but only he who does the will of my Father who is in heaven. Many will say to me on that day, 'Lord, Lord, did we not prophesy in your name, and in your name drive out demons and perform many miracles?' Then I will tell them plainly, 'I never knew you. Away from me, you evildoers!'" (Matt. 7:21–23).

Be warned, by Jesus himself, that just because Pope John Paul claimed they said something in Jesus' name as in one quote above, "Its authority in this matter [Tradition versus Scripture] is exercised in the name of Jesus Christ," doesn't mean Jesus or the Holy Spirit authorized what they said.

The Pope and his followers may have been able to prophecy, drive out demons, and perform many miracles, but that doesn't mean Jesus or the Holy Spirit were the authority behind these religious actions.

"I never knew you!"

"Away from me, you evil doers!"

If Jesus and the Holy Spirit were not the authority and power behind the miraculous deeds of false teachers such as mentioned in the Scripture quote above, then who was the power?

Some years ago I read this statement: "Demonism provides its own dynamic." What does that mean? It means that the demons under the devil's control have a certain power to accomplish wonder-working miracles.

The apostle Paul quoted the Holy Spirit with these words of caution, "The Spirit clearly says that in later times some will abandon the faith and follow deceiving spirits and things taught by demons. Such teachings come through hypocritical liars whose consciences have been seared as with a hot iron" (1 Tim. 4:1).

The apostle John adds these words on the same subject, "Dear friends, do not believe every spirit, but test the spirits to see whether they are from God, because many false prophets have gone out into the world" (1 John 4:1).

The only way anyone can test the spirits is by comparing and contrasting with the Scriptures what these demonic spirits teach.

In the following pages we will continue this very activity, comparing and contrasting the Scriptures with Catholic dogma. In the process, we will continue packing Scripture around the pillars of the Catholic religious system and anticipating the implosion of this demonic driven system.

THE SACRAMENTS EXPLAINED

CHAPTER 8 IS a kind of parenthesis. We are going to take the time to look a little deeper into the sacramental system. So far, we have looked at the fallacies surrounding four of the pillars: Peter, the popes, Mary, and Tradition. In chapter 9, we will get back to the structural pillars of Catholicism.

In the following, it may be easy to confuse what I am calling the seven pillars of Catholicism with Catholicism's seven sacraments. The seven pillars do not equate to the seven sacraments. For example, the four pillars Peter, the popes, Mary, and Tradition are not, as you will read, listed in the seven sacraments.

Now, let's look more closely at the sacraments.

As a result of Roman Catholics determining that their traditions were equal to Scripture, they also, at the Council of Trent, voted on just what those traditions would be and continue to be to this day. They call these rules, rites, and rituals sacraments.

Now, remember, Catholic Traditions are not taught in Scripture. The sacraments are rules, rites, and rituals created by Catholic leaders through which the Catholic faithful, by believing in and practicing these rules, rites, and rituals, would earn their way to heaven when they die.

The word *saved* (or to be saved) is the short version of determining that a person has submitted to all of the sacraments and is qualified to go to heaven.

The Catholics created seven sacraments which were, "Baptism, Confirmation or Chrismation, Eucharist, Penance, Anointing of the Sick, Holy Orders, and Matrimony."[1] It is by believing in and practicing these seven sacraments that a person is saved and will go to heaven.

The seven sacraments have been part of the Catholic religious system for hundreds of years during which Catholic believers trusted that their compliance with this sacramental religious system would get them to heaven, eventually. I say eventually because there was a large problem called purgatory standing in the way. Purgatory will be discussed in a later chapter.

The quotes that follow are either from the 1994 *Catholic Catechism* (previously cited) or from the Bible. Biblical quotes will be easily identified.

"Accordingly, just as Christ was sent by the Father so also he sent the apostles, filled with the Holy Spirit. This he did so that they might preach the Gospel to every creature and proclaim that the Son of God by his death and resurrection had freed us from the power of Satan and from death and brought us into the Kingdom of his Father. But he also willed that the work of salvation which they preached should be set in train through the sacrifice and sacraments around which the entire liturgical life revolves."[2]

Did you notice the phrase, "But he also willed"? Jesus Christ willed only two outward signs of faith and communion that those who believed in him and received him as their Savior should do: "And he took bread, gave thanks and broke it, and gave it to them, saying, 'This is my body given for you; do this in remembrance of me'" (Luke 22:19).

This was the first of the outward signs, or indicators that believers were ordered to do: communion (gathering together in a community of believers), as it is called among Protestants.

Baptizing believers with water was the only other outward indicator of one's belief that was commanded by Jesus. "All authority in heaven and on earth has been given to me. Therefore, go and make disciples of all nations, baptizing them in the name of the Father and of the Son and of the Holy Spirit" (Matt. 28:18–19).

In the above quote, note that "make disciples" comes before "baptizing."

The Scriptures can be searched high and low, but the above are the only two outward signifiers of belief and communion given by Jesus to his apostles to be taught to those who would believe in Jesus through their message.

However, there is one other command Jesus gave we should never forget: "A new command I give you: Love one another. As I have loved you, so you must love one another. By this all men will know that you are my disciples, if you love one another" (John 13:34–35).

As will be shown, neither of the indicators (communion and baptism) were commanded by Jesus as a means of salvation. Both water baptism and communion were to be experienced as results of salvation. More on this later.

If it would be helpful to you, review chapter 1, Becoming a Christian, as the true means of salvation, is explained there.

When the Catholics said that Jesus willed their seven sacraments, it is simply a statement they were forced to make (even though a lie). They had to say that Jesus willed the sacraments or they would have been left with no basis of authority for having made the sacraments into a religious system. There is no record in Scripture of Jesus willing their seven sacraments.

In the last quote above, it was also stated that Jesus, "willed that the work of salvation which they [the apostles] preached should be set in train through the sacrifice and sacraments." In other words, the sacraments are the way to salvation.

The word *sacrifice* mentioned above refers to the Eucharist, which is the culmination of the ritual called the Mass. This will be discussed in a later chapter as well as Holy Orders. Holy Orders is the process of becoming a priest and, by Catholic fiat, gaining the mystical power to change, for example, the bread and wine into the actual body and blood of Christ.

In the catechism it is further explained: "Thus the risen Christ, by giving the Holy Spirit to the apostles, entrusted to them his power of sanctifying: they became sacramental signs of Christ. By the power of the same Holy Spirit they entrusted this power to their successors. This 'apostolic succession' structures the whole liturgical life of the Church and is itself sacramental, handed on by the sacrament of Holy Orders."[3]

In the last quote, notice that the authority for the seven sacraments is now based upon apostolic succession. Chapters 2 through 5 of this book clearly showed there was no such thing as apostolic succession.

So, both sources of authority, Jesus willed it and apostolic succession, were clearly without any basis in Scripture. As the actor said in the dramatization, *Fiddler on the Roof,* "tradition, tradition, tradition." Tradition is all the Catholics can claim as a source of authority. We know what Jesus said about the traditions of men: "You hypocrites! Isaiah was right when he prophesied about you: 'These people worship me in vain; their teachings are but the rules taught by men'" (Matt 15:8–9).

And just as the Protestant Reformation forced the Catholics to determine if they were going to continue to equate their traditions with Scripture, the traditional religious system built upon the seven sacraments also had to be defended. It was not only "defended," against the Protestant teachers such as Luther, but, as we shall see, it was affirmed and fixed at the Council of Trent as the only means of being saved or getting to heaven.

The sacramental system was the superstructure Catholics erected upon the crumbled pillars of Peter as the first bishop of Rome (and the first pope), upon the whole structure of pope after pope, and upon Mary as a goddess.

In each case, whether in this chapter or other chapters, scriptural references will be included to show how these so called sacraments contradicted Scripture.

Where should we begin? It will be necessary to define what Catholics mean by the term *sacrament*.

Sacraments are "powers that come forth" from the Body of Christ, which is ever-living and life-giving. They are actions of the Holy Spirit at work in his Body, the Church. They are "the masterworks of God" in the new and everlasting covenant.[4]

The Church affirms that for believers the sacraments of the New Covenant are *necessary for salvation*. . . . "Sacramental grace" is the grace of the Holy Spirit, given by Christ and proper to each sacrament.[5]

The sacraments are efficacious signs of grace instituted by Christ and entrusted to the Church by which divine life is dispensed to us. The visible rites by which the sacraments are celebrated signify and make present the graces proper to each sacrament. They bear fruit in those who receive them with the required dispositions.[6]

By pulling out some of the phrases in the quotes above, we can get the sense of what is meant by sacraments.

Sacraments are "powers that come forth from the Body of Christ." Putting this statement in context, it says that water baptism, confirmation, Eucharist, Penance, Anointing of the Sick, Holy Orders, and Matrimony are powers that come forth from the body of Christ.

There is no Scripture offered to support the above statement.

What do the Scriptures say about power? Where does it come from? What is its purpose? In the apostle Paul's prayer for the church in Ephesus, he said these things about *power* (italicization is by this author):

> I pray that out of his glorious riches he may strengthen you *with power through his Spirit in your inner being*, so that Christ may dwell in your hearts through faith. And I pray that you, being rooted and established in love, may have *power* together with all the saints, to grasp how wide and long and high and deep is the love of Christ, and to know this love that surpasses knowledge—that you may be filled to the measure of all the fullness of God. Now to him who is able to do immeasurably more than all we ask or imagine, according to his power that is at work within us (Eph. 3:16–20).

What did Paul say to the church at Ephesus about power? This power:

1. Is to strengthen the believers

2. Comes through the Holy Spirit
3. Is applied to each believer's inner being
4. Is to enrich the believer's inner relationship with and trust in Christ
5. Is to be a shared power with all the saints (all believers)
6. Is to enable believers to understand how great the love of Christ is for each believer and to be filled full of God's love
7. Provides assurance by its presence within each believer; assurance that God is doing a work within the believer that goes beyond what can be imagined

If we were to study the concept of power as revealed throughout the New Testament, it would be clear to us that God is always the source of power in the believer and through the believer. Conversely, we would also find that power never comes from any religious acts generated from man's initiative, like doing the sacraments.

To say that the power of God comes from seven man-initiated sacraments or that the sacraments in and of themselves generate the power of God is heresy.

In the second statement from the Catholic *Catechism* quoted above, it said, "the sacraments . . . are *necessary for salvation.*"

In effect, Catholics are saying water baptism is necessary for salvation, or that marriage in the Catholic Church is necessary for salvation, or that Holy Orders is necessary for salvation.

If Holy Orders were necessary for salvation (it is only applied to bishops and priests), that would mean only bishops and priests go to heaven. That would exclude all the other Catholic faithful. If you were to read the eight-hundred-page catechism, you would find, as I did, numerous contradictions like this and numerous misrepresentations of Scripture.

In chapter 1 of this book, the way to become a Christian was carefully explained. But, the key ideas were:

1. For by grace are you saved through faith.
2. And it is not of yourselves.
3. It is the gift of God,
4. Not of any religious works,
5. So that no one can boast.
6. The believer is God's workmanship,
7. Created in Christ Jesus unto good works.

"Works" in the biblical context are not obedience to rules (laws) that one must do in order to be saved, or go to heaven, or have eternal life, or be accepted by any particular religious community. That is exactly what the seven sacraments of the Catholic religion are: laws; man-made rules, rites, and rituals.

Paul, the apostle, had these things to say about religious laws, and it must be understood, even though he is specifically referring to God's law, his statements apply to laws generated from any religious source: Catholicism, Mormonism, etc. "I do not set aside the grace of God, for if righteousness could be gained through the law, Christ died for nothing!" (Gal. 2:21)

Now that's a rather definitive statement: "Christ died for nothing." Following will be another statement from Paul for which there is also no counterargument.

> Therefore, there is now no condemnation for those who are in Christ Jesus, because through Christ Jesus the law of the Spirit of life set me free from the law of sin and death. For what the law [any religious law] was powerless to do in that it was weakened by the sinful nature, God did by sending his own Son in the likeness of sinful man to be a sin offering. And so he condemned sin in sinful man, in order that the

righteous requirements of the law [God's holy and just law, not the seven man-made sacraments of Catholicism] might be fully met in us, who do not live according to the sinful nature but according to the Spirit (Rom. 8:1–4).

True Christians "live . . . according to the Spirit." They don't live according to the seven sacraments of Catholicism or the religious laws of any other system.

Especially note in the above quote that, "Therefore, there is now no condemnation for those who are in Christ Jesus." "In Christ Jesus" is the underlying necessary condition. The underlying condition is not in subscribing to the Catholic religious system or to any other religious system be it Protestant, Catholic, or otherwise.

If any religious system is offering you rules, rites, or rituals as the means of salvation, they are not offering you Christ. Paul, in his letter to the Colossians, spoke eloquently of this truth. (Italicization is by this author.)

> I want you to know how much I am struggling for you and for those at Laodicea, and for all who have not met me personally. My purpose is that they may be encouraged in heart and united in love, so that they may have the full riches of complete understanding, in order that they may know the mystery of God, namely, Christ, in whom are hidden all the treasures of wisdom and knowledge. *I tell you this so that no one may deceive you by fine-sounding arguments* (Col. 2:1–4).

> So then, just as you received Christ Jesus as Lord, continue to live in him, rooted and built up in him, strengthened in the faith as you were taught, and overflowing with thankfulness. See to it that no one takes you *captive through hollow and deceptive philosophy, which depends on human tradition*

and the basic principles of this world rather than on Christ
(Col. 2:6–8).

Paul also said in his letter to the Romans something pre-
cisely definitive about grace and works. "And if [salvation is] by
grace, then it is no longer by works; if it were, grace would no
longer be grace" (Rom. 11:6).

If salvation is by grace, (the gift of God) there cannot be
works (the keeping of rules, rites, and rituals) because these two
spiritual principles are contradictory. Grace and doing religious
works (rules, rites, and rituals) in order to gain salvation are
mutually exclusive.

Paul made it clear when he said the believer is, "created in
Christ Jesus unto good works." If we are not created in Christ
Jesus, it is not possible for us to do good works. And even
if we are created in Christ Jesus, the good works that result
from God's life within us are not necessary to achieve salvation.
These good works are the result of salvation, by grace.

Now in the Catholic sacramental religious system, as quoted above, "sacraments are efficacious signs of grace." The word
efficacious according to Webster's dictionary means, "having the
power to produce a desired effect."

Logically, then, following Catholic reasoning, it is the sacraments that produce grace. In other words, grace is not efficacious without the seven sacraments.

If grace is a gift, and it is, then grace needs nothing to
make it efficacious. Let's say you just received a nice, brand
new sweater from a friend as a gift. What do you do to make it
useable? You put it on and wear it with thankfulness for your
friend.

The sweater is efficacious in its own right, simply by being a sweater. The receiver of the gift does nothing to make
the sweater efficacious. As the sweater, grace is efficacious in

its own right. It needs only to be received and put on. This is what the apostle Paul meant when he said, "You are all sons of God through faith in Christ Jesus, for all of you who were baptized into Christ have clothed yourselves with Christ" (Gal. 3:26–27).

And to the Romans, Paul said, "Let us behave decently, as in the daytime, not in orgies and drunkenness, not in sexual immorality and debauchery, not in dissension and jealousy. Rather, clothe yourselves with the Lord Jesus Christ, and do not think about how to gratify the desires of the sinful nature" (Rom. 13:13–14).

How is clothing ourselves with Christ and grace the same thing? Peter explained it quite well as he spoke to the assembly of elders in Jerusalem about his experience sharing the gospel with Gentiles. (Italicization by this author.) "God, who knows the heart, showed that he accepted them [Gentiles] by giving the Holy Spirit to them, just as he did to us [Jews]. He made no distinction between us and them, for he purified their hearts by faith. Now then, why do you try to test God by putting on the necks of the disciples a yoke that neither we nor our fathers have been able to bear? No! We believe it is *through the grace of our Lord Jesus that we are saved*, just as they are" (Acts 15:8–11).

"It is through the grace of our Lord Jesus." Grace comes because the Lord Jesus died on the cross for our sins and rose again from the dead for our justification (our righteousness).

In the above quote, what was the yoke that none of the Jews have been able to bear? Peter was referring to the law as given to Moses in the Old Testament. Just as the Jews could not bear that yoke, (they couldn't keep it perfectly), neither can anyone keep any religious system perfectly. Ask any Catholic if they keep all (their yoke) the rules, rites, and rituals of their religion perfectly.

Any system of religious laws, rules, rites, and rituals allows no failure.

You see, there can be no instance of failure to obey all of the requirements all of the time, not even one instance. James said in his letter, "For whoever keeps the whole law and yet stumbles at just one point is guilty of breaking all of it" (James 2:10). James is simply pointing out the nature of any religious system that depends upon keeping of laws: rules, rites, and rituals.

Paul makes it very clear that keeping religious laws, especially God's codified laws, are not efficacious for salvation: "Brothers, my heart's desire and prayer to God for the Israelites is that they may be saved. For I can testify about them that they are zealous for God, but their zeal is not based on knowledge. Since they did not know the righteousness that comes from God and sought to establish their own, they did not submit to God's righteousness. Christ is the end of the law so that there may be righteousness for everyone who believes" (Rom. 10:1–4).

To repeat, "Since they did not know the righteousness that comes from God and sought to establish their own, they did not submit to God's righteousness."

At the Council of Trent, Catholic leaders determinately sought to establish their own righteousness and did not submit to God's righteousness. They rejected the truth that salvation was, "by grace, through faith" (Eph. 2:8).

The person with this faith simply admits that there is nothing within himself/herself that could match up with the righteous requirements of a holy God. Salvation, then, is admission that there could be only one solution and that is the grace of God. Faith simply agrees with God and grabs onto the gift of grace.

At the Council of Trent, the decision makers totally rejected what is known as justification by faith. That is, the faith that grabs onto grace and will not let go and will not put any trust in its own merits, or anyone else's merits, but those of Jesus. It is faith in the total efficacy and completeness of the death and resurrection of Jesus the Christ. Otherwise, Jesus didn't need to die.

Remember that Paul said if any system of rules, rites, and rituals could save you, then Christ died in vain. At the Council of Trent, a religious system of rules, rites, and rituals was confirmed and fixed as the means of salvation. I'll say again, they established their own system of righteousness and obstinately rejected Christ as their Savior.

This obstinacy was maintained in the face of the outcries of biblical scholars and teachers such as Wycliffe, Hus, Zwingli, Luther, and Calvin. Parts of countries and entire countries under the leadership of Protestants had turned away from Catholicism. In spite of the biblical evidence offered by sincere men, the Catholic leaders at Trent simply rejected the Scriptures in favor of their own traditions.

What could we expect? A religious system that was based upon lies (Peter, Rome, popes, the rock, the keys, and Mary) could only continue on the basis of more lies. (Italicization in the passage that follows is this author's.)

> Jesus said to them, "If God were your Father, you would love me, for I came from God and now am here. I have not come on my own; but he sent me. Why is my language not clear to you? Because you are unable to hear what I say. *You belong to your father, the devil, and you want to carry out your father's desire. He was a murderer from the beginning, not holding to the truth, for there is no truth in him. When he lies, he speaks his native language, for he is a liar and the father of*

lies. Yet because I tell the truth, you do not believe me! Can any of you prove me guilty of sin? If I am telling the truth, why don't you believe me? He who belongs to God hears what God says. *The reason you do not hear is that you do not belong to God"* (John 8:42–47).

The Spirit clearly says that in later times some will abandon the faith and follow *deceiving spirits* and things *taught by demons.* Such teachings come through *hypocritical liars,* whose consciences have been seared as with a hot iron (1 Tim. 4:1–2).

I am making plain in this book that the Catholic religious system is based, from its very foundation, on lies. Where did those lies come from? Jesus said lies like this come from the devil. Paul said lies come from deceiving spirits and are taught by demons.

Paul also said, "Finally, be strong in the Lord and in his mighty power. Put on the full armor of God so that you can take your stand against the devil's schemes. For our struggle is not against flesh and blood, but against the rulers, against the authorities, against the powers of this dark world and against the spiritual forces of evil in the heavenly realms" (Eph. 6:10–12).

Christians who opposed the Roman Catholic religious system during the Protestant Reformation were at war (spiritual warfare) with the "powers of this dark world and against the spiritual forces of evil in the heavenly realms."

A friend made this comment after visiting the Vatican: "A few years ago, we visited the Vatican and one could not help but be filled with the spirit through the beautiful works of art, the great history there, and the magic that fellow travelers felt from being in this holy place."

As I read that message from my friend, I was reminded of what Paul said about spiritual warfare. Spiritual warfare is, "against the spiritual forces of evil in heavenly realms." Do you suppose Paul had in mind places like the Vatican when he used the term *heavenly realms?*

It is not the place itself with which we are at war. It is the spiritual, demonic forces that are driving the men and women of that place, which masquerades as a heavenly place.

We now have some understanding of the sacramental system and are ready to examine three more of the dogmas of that system. In the next chapter we will examine a foundational concept in the Catholic sacramental system: water baptism the fifth pillar.

Scriptural charges will be placed around this pillar (water baptism) of Catholicism as we build to the climax of the implosion of this evil system.

CHAPTER NINE

WATER BAPTISM

TO CONTINUE OUR examination of Catholicism's sacramental religious system, we will examine the first sacrament the Catholics offer as the way to salvation. Water baptism is the key or foundational sacrament. Catholics teach that water baptism opens the door to all the other sacraments.

Water baptism, therefore, is what I am identifying as the fifth structural pillar of the Catholic religious system.

"Holy [water] Baptism is the basis of the whole Christian life, the gateway to life in the Spirit . . . and the door which gives access to the other sacraments. Through Baptism we are freed from sin and reborn as sons of God; we become members of Christ, are incorporated into the Church and made sharers in her mission: 'Baptism is the sacrament of regeneration through water in the word.'"[1]

In the above quote, these astounding claims are made for water baptism:

1. The basis of the whole Christian life
2. The gateway to life in the Spirit (Holy Spirit)
3. The access to the other sacraments
4. The baptized person is freed from sin
5. The baptized person is reborn as a son of God
6. The baptized person is incorporated into the Catholic Church. By this statement, the Catholics mean that being baptized by a Catholic priest as a member of the Catholic Church was one of the laws (sacraments) that had to be obeyed.
7. The baptized person is started on the way to heaven by baptism in the Catholic Church—on the way only because there were six more sacraments.
8. Baptism is an act of regeneration.
9. The baptized person is justified by faith in water baptism.[2]
10. "Baptism seals the Christian."[3]

It is clear that the Catholic religious system places a lot of weight on water baptism: the whole Christian life depends upon it. The Holy Spirit won't work in one's life without water baptism, and one is freed from sin, born again, regenerated, justified, and sealed by water baptism.

It is also clear that what the Catholics want people to believe is that without being baptized by water in a Catholic church, none of the above results can happen.

And even after all of the assertions above, these contradictory statements about water baptism were made in the *Catechism*. "Baptism is birth into the new life in Christ. In accordance with the Lord's will, it is necessary for salvation."[4] Those who die for the faith, those who are catechumens, and all those who, without knowing of the Church [Catholic Church] but acting under the inspiration of grace, seek God sincerely and strive to fulfill his will, are saved even if they have not been baptized."[5]

So, we conclude from their own statement, to "seek God sincerely and strive to fulfill his will" is all that is required to be saved. Which is it, water baptism or seeking God sincerely? Or, neither!

It is time to look into the Scriptures to see just what the Lord and his followers taught about water baptism. The question is, of course, was water baptism necessary for salvation? Did water baptism carry the spiritual weight the Catholics claim for it: regeneration, justification, being born again, etc.?

In the New Testament, we quickly learn that there are three baptisms. The man known as John the Baptist said this of baptism: "I baptize you with water for repentance. But after me will come one who is more powerful than I, whose sandals I am not fit to carry. He will baptize you with the Holy Spirit and with fire" (Matt. 3:11).

In this book, being baptized with fire will not be discussed. However, it is well known that "fire" is a cleansing agent, a fierce, relentless destroyer of that which does not belong in a believer's life.

What will be discussed in the rest of this chapter is the relationship of water baptism to the baptism of the Holy Spirit. These baptisms are not comparable; they can only be contrasted. As we shall see, the baptism of the Holy Spirit is a necessary condition for salvation, while water baptism is only administered as evidence of salvation. The contrast is clearly made by John the Baptist in the quote above. The baptism of water for repentance was intended as a warning and wake-up call to the Jewish people. John makes it clear that his baptism with water was not sufficient. And we will see later in the book of Acts that the apostles made it clear that John's baptism of water for repentance was not sufficient.

Common sense tells us that being dipped under water (or having water poured on one's head) has no essential power to achieve anything. Anybody can submit to water baptism. Being dipped into a pool of water says nothing about the condition of the soul and spirit of the person being dipped.

There is a word the Catholics bring into the picture that you may be totally unfamiliar with. The word is *epiclesis*. The epiclesis are the actual words the priest says when baptizing a person. In the case of water baptism, the words are, "In the name of the Father, the Son, and the Holy Spirit."

Catholics are told that when the priest says those words, a bit of magic occurs. The water with which the person is being baptized magically becomes something other than water. The very character of the person being baptized changes: the priest by some extraordinary power he possesses (through the process called Holy Orders) changes the water into a magic potion. It's rather like a witch's brew. Only in this case, the priest doesn't have to stir the water, just say the magic words: "In the name of the Father, and the Son, and the Holy Spirit." It is not the words themselves, but the power possessed by the priest when he says the words.

I didn't use the term *witch's brew* lightly. Paul the apostle had something to say about witchcraft. "The acts of the sinful nature are obvious: sexual immorality, impurity and debauchery; idolatry and witchcraft" (Gal. 5:20).

Again, from the *Catechism* we read, "The essential rite of Baptism consists in immersing the candidate in water or pouring water on his head, while pronouncing the invocation [epiclecis] of the Most Holy Trinity: the Father, the Son, and the Holy Spirit."[6] "Baptism imprints on the soul an indelible spiritual sign, the character, which consecrates the baptized person for Christian worship. Because of the character Baptism cannot be repeated."[7]

"Because of the character" means that there was an actual change in the baptized person's state of being. "Baptism therefore constitutes *the sacramental bond of unity* existing among all who through it are reborn."

Let's look into the book of Acts and witness what Jesus said about the two baptisms: the baptism of the Holy Spirit and the baptism with water. "On one occasion, while he [Jesus] was eating with them, he gave them this command: 'Do not leave Jerusalem, but wait for the gift my Father promised, which you have heard me speak about. For John baptized with water, but in a few days you will be baptized with the Holy Spirit'" (Acts 1:4–5).

At this same meeting with his apostles, Jesus also said these words: "But you will receive power when the Holy Spirit comes on you" (Acts 1:8).

One of the things to notice was that the Holy Spirit was a gift that had been promised by God the Father. Being a gift, there is nothing to do but receive the gift when it is offered. If we were to read further in Acts, we would read that the Holy Spirit was given on the day of Pentecost, just as Jesus said.

The day of Pentecost was a major Jewish day of celebration. Jews from all over the area came to Jerusalem.

> When the day of Pentecost came, they [the apostles] were all together in one place. Suddenly a sound like the blowing of violent wind came from heaven and filled the whole house where they were sitting. They saw what seemed to be tongues of fire that separated and came to rest on each of them. All of them were filled with the Holy Spirit and began to speak in other tongues as the Spirit enabled them.

> Now there were staying in Jerusalem God-fearing Jews from
> every nation under heaven. When they heard this sound,
> a crowd came together in bewilderment, because each one
> heard them speaking in his own language. Utterly amazed,
> they asked: "Are not all these men who are speaking Gali-
> leans? Then how is it that each of us hears them in his own
> native language?" (Acts 2:1–8).

The above description is an account of the coming of the
Holy Spirit and the miracle that followed his coming. It is important to realize that it was the apostles (believers in Christ)
who were filled with the Holy Spirit. It was they who displayed
the miraculous speaking in the different languages of several of
the Jewish men who were at the day of Pentecost.

As the recorded history in the book of Acts continues, several incidents involving the Holy Spirit and water baptism oc-
cur. We must understand the book of Acts is not a theological
presentation, but a history of actual events. We will examine
two of these events: one involving Jews who believed in Christ
and the other involving Gentiles who believed. Beginning with
some Jews:

> Therefore, let all Israel be assured of this, God has made this
> Jesus, whom you crucified, both Lord and Christ. When
> the people heard this, they were cut to the heart and said to
> Peter and the other apostles, "Brothers, what shall we do?"
> Peter replied, "Repent and be baptized, every one of you,
> in the name of Jesus Christ for the forgiveness of your sins.
> And you will receive the gift of the Holy Spirit. The promise
> is for you and your children and for all who are far off—for
> all whom the Lord our God will call." With many other
> words he warned them; and he pleaded with them, "Save
> yourselves from this corrupt generation." Those who ac-
> cepted the message were baptized and about three thousand

were added to their number that day. They devoted themselves to the apostles' teaching and to the fellowship, to the breaking of bread and to prayer. Everyone was filled with awe, and many wonders and miraculous signs were done by the apostles (Acts 2:36–43).

Those Jewish brothers asked Peter, "What shall we do?" Peter responded, "Repent and be baptized, every one of you, in the name of Jesus Christ for the forgiveness of your sins. And you will receive the gift of the Holy Spirit." Those who accepted the message were baptized.

Peter's words, "repent and be baptized," give us some idea of the sequence of the spiritual choices that needed to be made: first, repentance and second, water baptism. Later in the passage, we are told, "Those who accepted the message were baptized." Again, the sequence is an act of acceptance (the, other side of the coin, so to speak, of repentance) and then water baptism.

Water baptism is a celebration of repentance (turning away from self and sin toward God) and acceptance of Jesus as one's Savior. Forgiveness of sins is an outcome of repentance and acceptance; it is not an outcome of getting baptized.

Peter also promised the "gift of the Holy Spirit." We can see how that promise was fulfilled in these words: "They [the new believers] devoted themselves to the apostles' teaching and to the fellowship, to the breaking of bread and to prayer. Everyone was filled with awe, and many wonders and miraculous signs were done by the apostles" (Acts 2:42–43).

Those new believers were immediately brought into a spiritual fellowship with the apostles and with one another. A church was born, and each one who had repented and accepted Christ Jesus were members of that church. Water baptism was the outward sign or indicator for each one of these new believers, and it meant the apostles were authorizing their right to be members of that fellowship.

In the above case, the Holy Spirit demonstrated his presence in some miraculous ways.

Let us note that there were no seven sacraments to follow. The apostles asked nothing of the audience but to repent, to accept the message, and water baptism was agreed upon as the means of confirming to those leaders the new believers' repentance and acceptance. The Holy Spirit set his seal upon this process by bringing them into a spiritual relationship with him and with one another.

Now we will examine the record of Peter's preaching the gospel to some Gentiles. Peter had been directed to go to a Gentile man named Cornelius and to tell him the message about Jesus. Following is the end result of Peter's preaching:

> While Peter was still speaking these words [Acts 10:43: that everyone who believes in him (Jesus) receives forgiveness of sins through his (Jesus') name], the Holy Spirit came on all who heard the message. The circumcised believers [Jews] who had come with Peter were astonished that the gift of the Holy Spirit had been poured out even on the Gentiles. For they heard them speaking in tongues and praising God. Then Peter said, "Can anyone [you fellow Jews] keep these people [Gentiles] from being baptized with water? They have received the Holy Spirit just as we have." So he ordered that they be baptized in the name of Jesus Christ (Acts 10:44–48).

Even though this was an entirely different racial group (Gentiles, not Jews), the sequence of belief and forgiveness of sins precedes water baptism. In this particular instance, the Holy Spirit is even more apparent as these new Gentile believers spoke in tongues. It is easy to understand why the Holy Spirit was more demonstrative with this group; they were Gentiles.

Notice in the text how the Jews who accompanied Peter were astonished that Gentiles received the gift of the Holy Spirit. The Holy Spirit made himself known in this demonstrative way so that the Jews would realize this gospel was meant for the whole world, not just for Jews.

Even with this kind of action on the part of the Holy Spirit, we know from other history that many Jews never really accepted that the Gentile believers were their brothers in Christ.

We could study through the entire book of Acts and find that there were instances of people believing in Jesus, but neither baptism by the Holy Spirit is mentioned, nor water baptism. We would find also that sometimes the Holy Spirit is mentioned in the record but not water baptism, and sometimes the exact opposite is recorded. This reality just reminds us to be very careful when we form our own belief about these two kinds of baptisms, and particularly, how we interpret texts of Scripture that are essentially history and not definitive theology.

When Paul and Barnabas were sent out on their first missionary excursion, there was not one mention of the Holy Spirit, or water baptism occurring as a result of their preaching. (Acts 13:1–14:25)

Paul, in his letters, said some interesting and instructive things about the baptism of the Holy Spirit, and water baptism. Regarding the baptism of the Holy Spirit: "The body is a unit, though it is made up of many parts; and though all its parts are many, they form one body. So it is with Christ. For we were all baptized by one Spirit into one body" (1 Cor. 12:12–13).

In the above verse, all believers in Christ are collectively referred to as a body. Throughout this passage, Paul uses the human body as an analogy to describe how any collective group (body) of Christians should function. But, the important idea to note here is that the believer is incorporated into Christ's body by being "baptized by one Spirit [Holy Spirit] into one body." It is not by water baptism as Catholics would have us believe. It is not being baptized into any church, including any Catholic church.

As Paul said in his letter to the Romans in chapter 8, verse 9, "You, however, are controlled not by the sinful nature but by the Spirit, if the Spirit of God lives in you. *And if anyone does not have the Spirit of Christ, he does not belong to Christ.*" (Italicization by this author.)

The presence of the Holy Spirit in a person's life is an absolute and necessary condition to being a Christian. It is the baptism of the Holy Spirit (placing the believer into the body of Christ) that seals the deal. It was further said by Paul: "And you also were included in Christ when you heard the word of truth, the gospel of your salvation. Having believed, you were marked in him with a seal, the promised Holy Spirit, who is a deposit guaranteeing our inheritance until the redemption of those who are God's possession—to the praise of his glory" (Eph. 1:13–14).

The promised Holy Spirit is himself the seal that confirms and guarantees the believer's salvation and eternal life. The seal is not water baptism!

The above quotes are the heart of the matter when it comes to being baptized with the Holy Spirit. But, Paul also wrote about water baptism in other places.

We will begin with one of the Catholics' favorite Scriptures that they use to prove that water baptism is necessary for salvation. "For in Christ all the fullness of the Deity lives in bodily form, and you have been given fullness in Christ, who is the head over every power and authority. In him you were also circumcised, in the putting off of the sinful nature, not with a circumcision done by the hands of men but with the circumcision done by Christ, having been buried with him in baptism and raised with him through your faith in the power of God, who raised him from the dead" (Col. 2:9–12).

Water baptism is a kind of dramatization of what happens to a person who believes in Christ. In another text, Paul put it this way: "I have been crucified with Christ and I no longer live, but Christ lives in me. The life [resurrected life] I live in the body, I live by faith in the Son of God, who loved me and gave himself for me" (Gal. 2:20).

The parallel thought in Colossians 2:9–12 is that the baptism of the Holy Spirit is not of human hands. Just like the circumcision Christ offers is not of human hands or human action. The baptism Paul speaks of here couldn't mean the circumcision the Jews practiced or water baptism, as both circumcision and water baptism is something men do with their hands.

Archibald Robertson, in his commentary, *Word Pictures in the New Testament*, wrote, "Paul does not mean to say that the new life in Christ is caused or created by the act of [water] baptism. That is grossly to misunderstand him."[9]

A.R. Fausett in the Jamieson, Fausett, and Brown commentary wrote "Baptism is the burial of the old carnal life, to which immersion symbolically corresponds." [10] As Fausett wrote, water baptism symbolically pictures an actual death and resurrection accomplished by the power of the Holy Spirit in the person who believes in Christ.

Just as circumcision for the Jews symbolically represented a cutting away of the flesh, so water baptism symbolizes the identification of the believer with Jesus' death and resurrection. The point is, water baptism is symbolic and has no power to achieve anything more than physical circumcision did for the Jew.

The issue of water baptism also came up in the course of Paul's ministry to the Gentiles.

> My brothers, some from Chloe's household have informed me that there are quarrels among you. What I mean is this: One of you says, "I follow Paul"; another, "I follow Apollos"; another, "I follow Cephas" [Peter]; still another, "I follow Christ." Is Christ divided? Was Paul crucified for you? Were you baptized into the name of Paul? I am thankful that I did not baptize any of you except Crispus and Gaius, so no one can say that you were baptized into my name. Yes, I also baptized the household of Stephanas; beyond that, I don't remember if I baptized anyone else. For Christ did not send me to baptize, but to preach the gospel—not with words of human wisdom, lest the cross of Christ be emptied of its power (1 Cor. 1:11–17).

The passage just quoted is instructive of Paul's attitude toward water baptism. It is easy to conclude Paul had no allusions about the importance of water baptism. To him, it wasn't important as to who did water baptism, nor was it important as an element of the message he was preaching as he went among the Gentiles.

Obviously, the Corinthians were influenced by their past religious experiences. There were cults in the Greco/Roman world that practiced baptisms as initiation rites. It was considered important to the initiate as to the rank and status of the person doing the baptizing. That is why some of the Corinthians were bragging about their being baptized by certain of the Christian leaders. There were arguments (bragging rights, we might say) among the Christians, and it was a divisive spirit in the church at Corinth.

Paul made it clear in this letter to the Corinthians that water baptism wasn't an essential feature of the gospel message. He further made the strong and definitive statement that it wasn't even part of the message Jesus sent him to preach: "lest the cross be emptied of its power."

Emptying the cross of its power is exactly what the Catholics have done with their emphasis on water baptism. We must understand that the cross loses its power when we allow anything else, like water baptism, to substitute for being crucified with Christ.

When Jesus comes into a person's life, he brings, in a sense, his cross with him. The believer goes onto that cross with Jesus. As Paul said, the believer is "crucified with Christ." That is why Jesus said that if a person believed in him, that person would, at that moment, pass from death unto life. The believer's lustful, sinful life is dead. The believer can now say, "I am dead, and my life is hid with Christ in God" It is a done deal. "For you died, and your life is now hidden with Christ in God. When Christ, who is your life, appears, then you also will appear with him in glory" (Col 3:3–4).

Because water baptism was, according to Catholic tradition, the gateway to salvation and every other one of their sacramental traditions, it seemed to me to require a thorough investigation. It is clear and without argument that water baptism is of no consequence in the actual salvation experience.

However, water baptism is of consequence. When a believer is baptized with water, he/she is declaring to the witnesses of that baptism that he/she believes in Jesus as Lord and Savior, and is publically identifying with Jesus in his death and resurrection. It needs to be clearly understood that the Scriptures teach that water baptism is an act demonstrating an already held faith in Jesus as Savior and Lord.

If the leading element of the sacramental system—water baptism—is based upon a blatant misuse of Scripture—dare I say, a lie—what about some of the other elements of the system?

The list of the seven sacraments contained two more pillars of the Catholic religious system.

We will continue preparing for the implosion as we pile up Scripture around these two foundational pillars.

In chapter 10, we will examine another extremely important structure in the system; the Eucharist.

CHAPTER 10

THE EUCHARIST

AT THE COUNCIL of Trent, among the seven sacraments that were settled upon and fixed in the doctrines of the Catholic religion, the Mass and Eucharist were undoubtedly the most significant.

In the book of Galatians, the apostle Paul made a troubling statement to that Gentile church he had planted.

> I am astonished that you are so quickly deserting the one who called you by the grace of Christ and are turning to a different gospel—which is really no gospel at all. Evidently some people are throwing you into confusion and trying to pervert the gospel of Christ. But even if we or an angel from heaven should preach a gospel other than the one we preached to you, let him be eternally condemned! As we have already said, so now I say again: If anybody is preaching to you a gospel other than what you accepted, let him be eternally condemned! (Gal. 1:6–9).

If you have read this book carefully up to this point, you must be convinced that the religion Catholics are preaching, teaching, and promoting is not the gospel.

Paul was not easy on the Galatians. He further said to them:

> You foolish Galatians! Who has bewitched you? Before your very eyes Jesus Christ was clearly portrayed as crucified. I would like to learn just one thing from you. Did you receive the [Holy] Spirit by observing the law, or by believing what you heard? Are you so foolish? After beginning with the Spirit, are you now trying to attain your goal by human effort? Have you suffered so much for nothing—if it really was for nothing? Does God give you his Spirit and work miracles among you because you observe the law, or because you believe what you heard? (Gal. 3:1–5)

Transposing what Paul said to the Galatians, and as we continue our investigation of the sacraments, especially the Mass and the Eucharist, we will see a religion based, not upon the grace of Christ and the Holy Spirit's work within each individual who believes, but on religious law (rules, rites, and rituals).

We will see, as we did when contrasting water baptism with the baptism of the Holy Spirit, just what Paul condemned in the Galatians when he asked them this question, "After beginning with the Spirit, are you now trying to attain your goal by human effort?" In the case of Catholicism, the "human effort" is the "law" of the seven sacraments.

And if you doubt that the Catholics consider the sacraments as law, here is what they said: (Italicization by this author): "Adhering to the teaching of the Holy Scriptures, to the apostolic traditions, and to the consensus . . . of the Fathers, we profess that 'the sacraments of *the new law* were . . . all instituted by Jesus Christ our Lord.'"[1]

The term *Mass* is a collective or umbrella term that refers to the entire content of this ritual. The content of the Mass is made up of two elements: the liturgy and the Eucharist.

Liturgy means all of the religious acts such as, prayer, singing, and reading prepared scripts. These liturgical acts and procedures lead up to the grand finale, the Eucharist. The Eucharist has its own prepared liturgy that brings the priest to offer to God the sacrifice of Christ (a bit of bread and a cup of wine) that in some superstitious, mystical, and miraculous way has been changed into the actual body and blood of Jesus.

It is important to note that the Eucharist is considered a sacrifice. "The *Holy Sacrifice,* because it makes present the one sacrifice of Christ the Savior and includes the Church's offering. The terms *holy sacrifice of the Mass, sacrifice of praise, spiritual sacrifice, pure and holy sacrifice* are also used, since it completes and surpasses all the sacrifices of the Old Covenant.[2]

In the above quote, there is a statement regarding the superiority of the Eucharist. It is said, "Since it completes and surpasses all the sacrifices of the Old Covenant." The Old Covenant was, of course, referring to the sacrificial laws of the Old Testament. We will see in the following that this is a perversion of what is said in the Scriptures about he who actually surpasses the sacrifices of the Old Testament once and for all time. "Such a high priest [referring to Jesus] meets our need—one who is holy, blameless, pure, set apart from sinners, exalted above the heavens. Unlike the other high priests, he does not need to offer sacrifices day after day, first for his own sins, and then for the sins of the people. He sacrificed for their sins once for all when he offered himself. For the law appoints as high priests men who are weak; but the oath which came after the law, appointed the Son, who has been made perfect forever" (Heb. 7:26–28).

It is Jesus who meets our need. He met it once for all. There is no more offering of sacrifices day after day as in the Eucharist.

The Eucharist, a superstitious, mystical, and miraculous event is supposedly made possible by the priest (or bishop) saying some magic words called the epiclesis. It must be the priest who says these words. It is the priest by virtue of his Holy Orders who has the power to turn the bread and wine into Jesus' actual body and blood.

To apply the above statement from Hebrews, the priests of the Catholic religion are priests "who are weak." They are weak and they are going to die because they are mere humans just like the rest of us sinners.

That is not all. There is no such thing as Holy Orders. This term, or the concept it defines, is nowhere in the Bible. No human being has the power to change a piece of bread and a cup of wine into the actual body and blood of Jesus. As was said before, it is simply superstition, mysticism, and magic.

The picture that comes to my mind is a witch standing over a pot of bubbling liquid saying some mumbo jumbo (the epiclesis) as the liquid becomes a poisonous elixir.

> In the *epiclesis* the Church [actually the priest who is presiding over the sacrifice] asks the Father to send his Holy Spirit (or the power of his blessing) on the bread and wine, so that by his power they may become the body and blood of Jesus Christ and so that those who take part in the Eucharist may be one body and one spirit.[3]

> In the *institution narrative*, the power of the words and the action of Christ, and the power of the Holy Spirit, make sacramentally present under the species of bread and wine

Christ's body and blood, his sacrifice offered on the cross once for all.[4]

She [the Church and the priest on behalf of the Church] presents to the Father the offering [sacrifice] of his Son which reconciles us with him.[5]

The change that supposedly occurs in the bread and wine is called *transubstantiation*. That's a big word, and it carries a lot of religious heresy within it. We will trace the history of this heresy clear back to the time of the philosopher, Aristotle. Even though Aristotle didn't know it, his thoughts on *substance* and *accidents* would become a foundation for justifying this Catholic heresy.

Aristotle lived before the time of Christ. But what he said about the nature of existence somehow explains transubstantiation, as Diarmaid MacCulloch, in his book, *The Reformation: A History*, attempts to explain the process to us.

Aristotle divided the being of a particular object into substance and accidents. Take a sheep, for instance: its substance, which is its reality, its participation in the universal quality of being a sheep, is manifested in its gamboling on the hills, munching grass and baaing. Its accidents are things particular to the individual sheep at which we are looking: the statistics of its weight, the curliness of its wool, or the timbre of its baa. When the sheep dies, it ceases to gambol on the hills, munch grass and baa: its substance, its "sheepiness," is instantly extinguished, and only the accidents remain—its corpse, including its weight, curly wool or voice box—and they will gradually decay. They are not significant to its former sheepiness, which has ended with the extinguishing of its substance in death. It is no longer a sheep.[6]

Did you get that? MacCulloch followed with an explanation of how Aristotle's theory of substance and accidents translates into transubstantiation.

> How, as scholastics [theologians who took the writings of the philosophers and fathers of the Church as the truth] following Aquinas's method, might we apply what is true of a sheep to the miracle of the Mass? We start with bread (we could equally start with wine). Bread consists of substance and accidents: its substance is in participation in the universal quality of "breadness," while its accidents are the particular appearance of this piece of bread (being round, white and wafer-like, for instance). In the Mass, substance changes, accidents do not—why should they? They are not significant for being. Through the grace of God, the substance of bread is replaced by the substance of the Body of Christ.[7]

Notice the conclusion contained in the last sentence: "Through the grace of God, the substance of bread is replaced by the substance of the Body of Christ." It is the grace of God that causes this magic to happen. So, now, God is involved in this bit of witchcraft.

MacCulloch went on to explain that Thomas Aquinas was the Catholic philosopher who took Aristotle's theory of substance and accidents and applied it in a way that he claimed justified transubstantiation. I don't think you will be impressed. "It is a satisfying and reverent analysis: as long, that is, as one accepts Thomas's scientific or philosophical premises of the language of substance and accidents, affirming the conception of universal realities which are greater than individual instances, such as the reality of being as sheep or being bread, rather than particular instances of sheep or bread."[8]

Well now, there it is, the explanation of transubstantiation. Are you impressed?

Was it "satisfying and reverent" to you? It's gobbledygook, and there is no other word for it. It is the foundation and justification for the mumbo jumbo expressed by the priest in the epiclesis. Thomism, as it was called, became a significant contributor to the Council of Trent. "Numerous Thomists took part in the preparatory work for the Council of Trent."[9]

As was said before, it was at the Council of Trent when transubstantiation (the Eucharist) was fixed as Catholic doctrine.

MacCulloch also points out that a new philosophy called Nominalism rose up to challenge the whole concept of substance and accidents. Nominalists said a sheep is just that, a sheep, and bread is bread. Along came the Protestant reformers and pointed out transubstantiation was not a scriptural concept, and that Catholics believed this myth only because Catholic authorities said it was true. Some Protestants lost their lives as a result of their open disagreement.[10]

Transubstantiation is very important to the theory of the Eucharist. But, more importantly for the purposes of this discussion, the Eucharist is a pillar (the sixth pillar) of the Catholic religious structure and system.

Just to be clear, transubstantiation is the mysterious process that causes the bread and wine to be Jesus, and the Eucharist is the sacrifice of this transubstantiated Jesus; it is sacrificing Jesus over and over again every time there is a Mass.

Unfortunately, it wasn't just the theories of Aristotle and Aquinas that were used to justify transubstantiation. The Catholic interpretation of two passages of Scripture which are the incident of the Last Supper recorded in the gospels of Matthew,

Mark, and Luke, plus John's gospel, chapter 6, are used by Catholics to authenticate the sacrifice of the Eucharist.

Because the words of Scripture under discussion are virtually identical in Matthew, Mark, and Luke, we will use only Luke's record as the basis of our examination. Luke's rendition is in Luke, chapter 22.

In general, the historical situation (context) of the Last Supper was to remember and to celebrate the Day of Unleavened Bread. Associated with that day of celebration in the Jewish religious experience was the sacrifice of the Passover lamb.

When John the Baptist, at one of his times of baptizing, "saw Jesus passing by, he said, 'Look, the Lamb of God!'" (John 1:36).

Of course, Jesus as the Lamb of God is a direct and clear fulfilling of the Old Testament type, the Passover Lamb. We must keep this in mind as we examine and correctly interpret what Jesus said about his body and blood.

We must keep in mind also, that the Passover was an act of remembering. Jews had been remembering this day of the Passover for centuries. So, when Jesus said in the following quote, "do this in remembrance of me," he was simply asking them to follow the historical precedent of remembering the sacrifice of his body and blood as the Jews had been doing for centuries.

Picking up the story in Luke's gospel:

Jesus sent Peter and John, saying, "Go and make preparations for us to eat the Passover." "Where do you want us to prepare for it?" they asked.

He replied, "As you enter the city, a man carrying a jar of water will meet you. Follow him to the house that he enters, and say to the owner of the house, 'The Teacher asks: Where is the guest room, where I may eat the Passover with my disciples?' He will show you a large upper room, all furnished.

Make preparations there." They left and found things just as Jesus had told them. So they prepared the Passover.

When the hour came, Jesus and his apostles reclined at the table. And he said to them, "I have eagerly desired to eat this Passover with you before I suffer. For I tell you, I will not eat it again until it finds fulfillment in the kingdom of God."

After taking the cup, he gave thanks and said, "Take this and divide it among you. For I tell you I will not drink again of the fruit of the vine until the kingdom of God comes."

And he took bread, gave thanks and broke it, and gave it to them, saying, "This is my body given for you; do this in remembrance of me."

In the same way, after the supper he took the cup, saying, "This cup is the new covenant in my blood, which is poured out for you" (Luke 22:8–20).

It is the last two verses (19 and 20) that have caused so much discussion, bickering, and even terror over many centuries. The Catholics, as has been explained above, take the phrases "This is my body" and "This cup is the new covenant in my blood" to mean that Jesus meant, literally, the bread and the wine were his actual body.

Now it is obvious Jesus hadn't meant this to be taken literally. He is sitting right in front of them in his body. How could he have meant, other than by analogy, that the bread and the wine were his body and blood?

When the Scriptures make plain sense, seek no other sense.

Jesus said in verse 22, "The Son of Man will go as it has been decreed." The suffering on the cross had been decreed. That is, it had been planned at the time the creation of this world was initiated as the following text tells us. "All inhabitants of the earth will worship the beast—all whose names have not been written in the book of life belonging to the Lamb that was slain from the creation of the world" (Rev. 13:8).

It was the mutilation and blood spilling leading to his death that the disciples (and you and I) were to remember. We who believe are to remember that Jesus was slain for us—he paid the price for our sins.

"Do this in remembrance of me." Just as the Jews, for centuries, had remembered the Passover lamb by a celebration once each year, Jesus' followers were to remember Jesus as their true Passover Lamb at times when they gathered in community for a meal and fellowship. It was to remember his sacrifice, not to sacrifice him over and over again as in the so called Eucharist.

> For Christ did not enter a man-made sanctuary that was only a copy of the true one; he entered heaven itself, now to appear for us in God's presence; Nor did he enter heaven to offer himself again and again, the way the high priest enters the Most Holy Place every year with blood that is not his own. Then Christ would have had to suffer many times since the creation of the world. But now he has appeared once for all at the end of the ages to do away with sin by the sacrifice of himself. Just as man is destined to die once, and after that to face judgment, so Christ was sacrificed once to take away the sins of many people; and he will appear a second time, not to bear sin, but to bring salvation to those who are waiting for him (Heb. 9:24–28).

Before we move on, it is notable that the disciples asked not one question about what Jesus meant in the above two verses about the bread and the cup. Apparently, they understood Jesus' meaning. They probably didn't understand totally, but they must have understood Jesus was using the bread and wine as an analogy. It made plain sense to them, just as it makes plain sense to you and me.

We will see in the following text, the apostle Paul's description of how the churches were learning to live out this particular command of Jesus (Remember me), that there were difficulties. But, these difficulties were not in any way associated with misunderstanding the meaning of the bread and wine.

In the following directives I have no praise for you, for your meetings do more harm than good. In the first place, I hear that when you come together as a church, there are divisions among you, and to some extent I believe it. No doubt there has to be differences among you to show which of you have God's approval [seemingly a type of one-upmanship].

When you come together, it is not the Lord's Supper you eat, for as you eat, each of you goes ahead without waiting for anybody else. One remains hungry, another gets drunk. Don't you have homes to eat and drink in? Or do you despise the church of God and humiliate those who have nothing? What shall I say to you? Shall I praise you for this? Certainly not!

For I received from the Lord what I also passed on to you: The Lord Jesus, on the night he was betrayed, took bread, and when he had given thanks, he broke it and said, "This is my body, which is for you; do this in remembrance of me." In the same way, after supper he took the cup, saying, "This cup is the new covenant in my blood; do this, whenever you drink it, in remembrance of me." For whenever you eat this bread and drink this cup, you proclaim the Lord's death until he comes.

Therefore, whoever eats the bread or drinks the cup of the Lord in an unworthy manner will be guilty of sinning against the body and blood of the Lord. A man ought to examine himself before he eats of the bread and drinks of the cup. For anyone who eats and drinks without recognizing the body of the Lord eats and drinks judgment on himself. That is why many among you are weak and sick, and a number of you have fallen asleep [died]. But if we judged ourselves, we would not come under judgment. When we are judged by the Lord, we are being disciplined so that we will not be condemned with the world.

So then, my brothers, when you come together to eat, wait for each other. If anyone is hungry, he should eat at home, so that when you meet together it may not result in judgment (1 Cor. 11:17–34).

The clear intent of this passage is to correct the "unworthy manner" of the believers when they got together for a meal that involved what Protestants call *communion*. It was not just to correct the unruly behavior, but it was to warn them that if they didn't correct that behavior, they may experience certain kinds of judgment. Indeed, they had already experienced sicknesses and some had died.

However, we must note that there was no confusion among these believers about the bread and the cup. There was no religious ritual associated with remembering the Lord's death. It was remembered in the context of a simple meal. The bread and the cup were, in some way, we are not told, celebrated as a part of the meal.

This group of believers had no sense, apparently, of the seriousness of taking bread and wine in an act of remembrance of the death of their Savior. It was not to be party time. Paul never mentions, or even hints at, the bread and cup being in some way transformed into the real body and blood of Jesus.

Paul claims to have received directly from the Lord Jesus himself the instruction he gives to the Corinthian church. Doesn't it seem reasonable that if Jesus gave Paul these instructions about how to remember him, that he would have included an explanation that the bread and the cup were really his body and blood? The idea is so esoteric and unbelievable that Jesus would have had to explain it all to Paul. Obviously, it wasn't part of what Jesus taught Paul.

Should we believe Jesus and Paul, or should we believe the absolutely incredible and imaginary tale propagated by Catholics?

Taking communion was serious business; not doing it in the proper manner (to borrow Paul's expression) meant sickness and death. So, for Jesus not to explain to Paul about the bread and cup being his real body to be offered over and over again as a sacrifice would have been a serious breech on Jesus' part. How could Jesus have not included that instruction to Paul, and if Paul had received it, why didn't he tell the Corinthians?

It is only the Catholics who have invented this heresy. There is no justification for it. They tried to bring in a worldly philosopher's gobbledygook about substance and accidents to support the theory. But that philosophy when applied to the bread and the cup is just so much foolishness. And, then, as we have read, they took Jesus' own words about the bread and the cup and invented a meaning and application called the Eucharist that has no scriptural warrant.

But they weren't through with Scripture yet. The pressure was on. The Nominalist philosophers weren't buying transubstantiation, and the Protestant leaders were beginning to speak out against it. Catholics needed to come up with more justification; specifically, justification for the theory of transubstantiation.

Their need leads us to an examination of John's gospel, chapter 6. Jesus made an incredible statement. He said to a group of Jews:

"I tell you the truth, unless you eat the flesh of the Son of Man and drink his blood, you have no life in you. Whoever eats my flesh and drinks my blood has eternal life, and I will raise him up at the last day. For my flesh is real food and my blood is real drink. Whoever eats my flesh and drinks my blood remains in me, and I in him. Just as the living Father sent me and I live because of the Father, so the one who feeds on me will live because of me. This is the bread that came down from heaven. Your forefathers ate manna and died, but he who feeds on this bread will live forever." He said this while teaching in the synagogue in Capernaum (John 6:53–59).

On the surface, the above text seems to vindicate the Catholic's contention that the believer has to eat Jesus body and drink his blood. But let's follow the story and we will see that interpretation doesn't hold up.

Can you imagine saying to a group of Jews in a Jewish synagogue that they had to eat the flesh of a dead man and drink his blood? Jews were forbidden to drink blood, and they weren't allowed to even touch a dead body. One result of Jesus' words was that, "From this time many of his disciples turned back and no longer followed him" (John 6:66).

Jesus said (verse 61) to those who were considering dropping out, "Does this offend you?" Certainly it offended them. Jesus knew that it would. In verse 64, it is said, "For Jesus had known from the beginning which of them did not believe and who would betray him." It was no surprise to Jesus that many of the Jews walked away. Who wouldn't if Jesus' words about eating his flesh and drinking his blood were to be taken literally?

What would you think if some religious leader told you that you had to eat his flesh and drink his blood? Just by asking and answering that question, it is obvious Jesus didn't mean this to be taken literally. If it makes plain sense; seek no other sense.

Jesus went on to ask his disciples, "You do not want to leave too, do you?" Jesus asked the Twelve.

"Simon Peter answered him, "Lord, to whom shall we go? You have the words of eternal life. We believe and know that you are the Holy One of God" (John 6:67–69).

Peter knew Jesus wasn't speaking literally about eating his flesh and drinking his blood. He doesn't even mention that idea in his response to Jesus. It was ridiculous to think Jesus meant those words literally. However, that is just what the Catholics want us to believe.

Jesus also said to those who eventually departed from him, but he meant them for us, too, "The words I have spoken to you are spirit and they are life" (John 6:63).

Those words about eating his flesh and drinking his blood were "spirit." What did Jesus mean by that? Just before Jesus said, "The words I have spoken to you are spirit," he said, "The Spirit gives life; the flesh counts for nothing." Jesus told them that the words he spoke were meant to be understood in spiritual terms, not in terms of the human body, the material body, or of the body of flesh.

The apostle Paul helps us understand the difference in flesh and spirit. "The mind of sinful man is death, but the mind controlled by the Spirit is life and peace; the sinful mind is hostile to God" (Rom. 8:6).

In the case of the Jews who interpreted Jesus' words literally and "turned back and no longer followed him," their minds interpreted Jesus' words in a way that would lead to their spiritual death. Their minds were not controlled by the Spirit, and they were hostile to God. They took it literally. They walked away.

On the other hand, Peter knew there was a deeper, spiritual meaning to Jesus' words, and responded accordingly: "We believe and know that you are the Holy One of God."

There is another concept the Catholics tied into the Eucharist that is a terrible error. They called it, "the real presence." (Italicization by this author.)

> Christians come together in one place for the Eucharistic assembly. At its head is Christ himself, the principal agent of the Eucharist. He is high priest of the New Covenant; *it is he himself who presides invisibly over every Eucharistic celebration.* [11]

> We carry out this command of the Lord by celebrating the *memorial of his sacrifice.* In so doing, *we offer to the Father* what he has himself given us: the gifts of his creation, bread and wine which, by the power of the Holy Spirit and by the words of Christ, *have become the body and blood of Christ. Christ is thus really and mysteriously made present.* [12]

> In the most blessed sacrament of the Eucharist "the body and blood, together with the soul and divinity, of our Lord Jesus Christ and, therefore, *the whole Christ is truly, really, and substantially* contained." "This presence is called 'real'—by which is not intended to exclude the other types of presence as if they could not be 'real' too, but because it is presence in the fullest sense: that is to say, it is a *substantial* presence by which *Christ, God and man, makes himself wholly and entirely present.*" [13]

> *It is Christ himself,* the eternal high priest of the New Covenant who, acting through the ministry of the priests, *offers the Eucharistic sacrifice.* And it is *the same Christ, really present under the species of bread and wine, who is the offering of the Eucharistic sacrifice.*[14]

All of the above points out one incredible aspect of the Eucharist; that Jesus is there offering himself on the altar in the piece of bread and the wine. How could anyone in their right mind believe this bit of magic? Of course, the Catholics like to call this whole bit of hocus pocus a mystery. Calling it a mystery gets them off the hook. It doesn't have to be rational.

The Scriptures make it very clear where and in whom Jesus is present.

Here I am! I stand at the door and knock. If anyone hears my voice and opens the door, I will come in and eat with him, and he with me (Rev. 3:20).

Jesus replied, "If anyone loves me, he will obey my teaching. My Father will love him, and we will come to him and make our home with him (John 14:23).

Don't you know that you yourselves are God's temple and that God's Spirit lives in you? (1 Cor. 3:16)

Do you not know that your body is a temple of the Holy Spirit, who is in you, whom you have received from God? You are not your own; you were bought at a price. Therefore, honor God with your body (1 Cor. 6:19–20).

If you love me, you will obey what I command. And I will ask the Father, and he will give you another Counselor to be with you forever—the Spirit of truth. The world cannot accept him, because it neither sees him nor knows him. But you know him, for he lives with you and will be in you (John 14:15–17).

So then, just as you received Christ Jesus as Lord, continue to live in him, rooted and built up in him, strengthened in

the faith as you were taught, and overflowing with thankfulness (Col. 2:6–7).

> Now I rejoice in what was suffered for you, and I fill up in
> my flesh what is still lacking in regard to Christ's afflictions,
> for the sake of his body, which is the church. I have become
> its servant by the commission God gave me to present to you
> the word of God in its fullness—the mystery that has been
> kept hidden for ages and generations, but is now disclosed to
> the saints. To them God has chosen to make known among
> the Gentiles the glorious riches of this mystery, which is
> Christ in you, the hope of glory (Col. 1:24–27).

Christ is not in a piece of bread and a cup of wine. Christ
is in you (the believer).

As the verses above tell us, Christ is in the believer, the
Father is in the believer, and the Holy Spirit is in the believer.
"Don't you know that you yourselves are God's temple?" This
reality is the only "hope of glory."

As Paul said to the Colossians, "See to it that no one takes
you captive through hollow and deceptive philosophy [tran-
substantiation, for example], which depends on human tradition and the basic principles of this world rather than on
Christ" (Col. 2:8).

In the next chapter, we will examine the concept of purgatory and related doctrines. Purgatory (that is, to escape purgatory) is one of the reasons why the seven sacraments were created by Catholic theologians.

Just as the Eucharist, the reader will see that purgatory is
also a shameful doctrine and is the seventh pillar of the Catholic religious system.

At the end of the following chapter, we will be at the point
of implosion.

CHAPTER 11

PURGATORY: THE GREAT PONZI SCHEME

IF THE BIBLE is read carefully and under the influence of the Holy Spirit, it is very clear that God calls certain believers to the role of leadership in the body of Christ; particularly in individual churches.

However, there is one other thing that is very clear in the Scriptures; God calls certain people to be leaders but not lords.

The apostle Paul could easily have taken the position of lordship and not leadership. But here is what he had to say to the church at Corinth, "I call God as my witness that it was in order to spare you that I did not return to Corinth. Not that we lord it over your faith, but we work with you for your joy, because it is by faith you stand firm" (2 Cor. 1:23–24).

As you have read this book up to this point, it must have been clear that Catholic leaders have that exact intention: to lord it over the people under their religious tutelage.

Every doctrine or decree has as its fundamental intent, lordship. This lordship even extends to popes demanding infallibility. They, in this vein of lordship, even claim apostolic primacy: I'm top dog. I'm the Vicar of Christ. I rule.

As you read the rest of this chapter, remember there is no such position in the Christian heritage as that of a pope.

But Catholic lordship, even though it begins with a phony pope, doesn't end with the pope.

In the Catholic religious system, bishops and priests lord it over their districts and congregations. The Catholic faithful must confess their sins to a priest and endure whatever penance is prescribed to ensure forgiveness. The faithful must worship in exactly the manner prescribed for them by the bishop or priest. These acts of worship (sacraments) are only efficacious if the bishop or priest says the magic words (the epiclesis). They must believe in and follow the seven sacraments under the eye of the local bishop or priest, or they won't be saved. And even if saved, at death they must pass through a state of existence called purgatory. They must go through purgatory in order to be cleansed of all their sins that didn't get taken care of while on earth.

In this system of lordship, God help the Catholic who doesn't get final absolution from a bishop or priest (or last rites) at the time of death. Absolution is supposedly that moment just before death when the priest forgives the dying person of all their sins. It might be asked, "If absolution takes care of all the person's sins, then what is the need for purgatory?"

The answer to that question will be apparent in the following discussion.

The purpose of lordship is essentially to establish a state of religious fear and thus to have control of the faithful Catholic's life. Purgatory was invented by Catholic leaders for that very purpose: control through fear.

The following explanation is only a simile, but no simile will have an exact correspondence with what it is being compared. Purgatory is like a Ponzi scheme.

As far as is known, Charles A. Ponzi (an Italian-born American) was the first man to have used this money-making method. Ponzi was a swindler whose system was picked up by a number of other crooks.

For example, in recent years here in the United States, a man named Bernie Madoff cheated hundreds, perhaps thousands, of people out of millions of dollars. Some of the most prominent people in America were victims of Bernie's Ponzi scheme. Many retired people lost their life savings by investing in this system of—using Luther's term—"the cheat."

In a Ponzi scheme, the perpetrator convinces investors to give him some or all of their monetary assets. They give their assets because the perpetrator promises that he can invest their money at a much higher rate than the victim can get in the regular marketplace. The investor gives his money over expecting to receive a very lucrative return on his investment. And he does receive, in the first few months, even years, the expected high return. In fact, the return is so great that he might even decide to invest more, and this does happen in many cases.

What the perpetrator has been doing is using the committed investor's money to pay the high dividends to new investors. It is, as the saying goes, a house of cards. The whole thing crashes when it is either discovered by federal authorities or several investors, who, at the same time, decide they want their money back. When several investors want their money back at the same time, it's usually because they, as the saying goes, "smell a rat." Or, it might be simply because they now need the money.

The Ponzi man can't pay up because the money is all out there paying those high dividends to new investors, getting them hooked. And he has been spending a lot of that money on himself; in the case of the popes, building cathedrals, and buying expensive properties for themselves, etc. What they did with the money that came into their treasury need not be detailed. It is in all of the history books.

But, you will remember that Luther's original complaint was due to the fact a pope was promising years off of purgatory if people would invest in building a cathedral for Peter.

You might ask, "Why did the Pope want to build this cathedral?" The purpose was to have this grandiose monument that would attract worshippers to come to Rome to spend their money and to fall into the trap of considering Rome and the pope as a super holy place. Pilgrims would receive special blessings, their sins forgiven, miraculous healings, etc. It is all in the history books.

As the Moslems going on a pilgrimage to their so called holy sites assures them of great religious blessings, millions still go to Rome for the same reasons.

In the coming pages, you will read just how the Catholic religious system, through the concept of purgatory, promises a sure passage (although a delayed passage) to heaven. Millions of people over the centuries have invested in the promised passage through purgatory but have no idea if the payoff will ever come. They don't even know for sure if purgatory is real.

A prominent Roman Catholic media icon recently stated on his television show that when he died, all of his assets (it is assumed he meant after his family would be taken care of) will go to charity. The following is not an exact quote, but it certainly captures the essence of what he said. "I'm counting this will me get into heaven." He meant, of course, that he was attempting to buy his way into heaven. Then, as a kind of afterthought, this Catholic man said, "I hope."

I couldn't help but think that what this Catholic said was an example of just what I'm exposing in this chapter. But, it is not just Catholics who want to buy their way into heaven. In a recent *Los Angeles Times* sports page, a worldwide revered athlete—a Moslem—apparently said to his wife numerous times, "I just want to get to heaven, and I've got to do a lot of good deeds to get there."

If you have any doubt that neither money, nor good deeds will buy your way into heaven, please read chapter 1 again.

The Catholic media icon never used the term *purgatory*, but there is no doubt that is what was on his mind. I've heard that some Catholics say they don't believe in purgatory anymore. As you read the following pages, you will see that purgatory still is an official Catholic dogma.

For the Catholic, their time in this life hangs under the threat that it might take them years in purgatory to have their debt of sin paid off. So, they must pile up as many points (invest in purgatory) as they can while here on earth. Of course, the Catholic leaders have figured out a scheme to sell to the people: the promise of a huge payoff (making it through purgatory sooner) depending upon of course, how much is invested now. This evil scheme will reveal itself in the coming pages.

Diarmaid MacCulloch, in his book *The Reformation: A History*, describes the system of purgatory is these ways: (Italicization by this author.)

> But while the Mass was at the centre of *this burgeoning industry* of intercession, plenty of other commodities could be traded for years in Purgatory—literally traded in the case of indulgence grants. . . . The Church told them that there was

a great deal of merit available, if *only it was drawn on with reverence and using the means provided by the Church.*

Works such as these could then form part of *a spiritual trade* within the community of the living for another form of good work—prayer. So the beggar was expected to pray for the future welfare of the soul of the good wife who gave him a coin, the inmates of the hospitals must lie in their beds praying for their benefactors. . . . Every soul-prayer could bear on one's time in Purgatory. Better still, to pray for the souls of the dead was also mutually beneficial, because the dead in Purgatory, with a good deal of time on their hands, could be expected to reciprocate with their own prayers.

No wonder Purgatory was one of the most successful and long-lasting theological ideas in the Western Church [Catholic Church], *or bred an intricate industry* of prayer.[1]

MacCulloch saw the whole system for what it was, an "industry." He also had this to say in his book, *Christianity: The First Three Thousand Years*, "What was worse, the Church had taken God's sacraments and turned them into part of an elaborate confidence trick on God's people. Luther proclaimed his message to all the victims of the cheat." [2]

Is purgatory, indulgences and such, the confidence trick Peter referred to when he wrote: "But there were also false prophets among the people, just as there will be false teachers among you. They will secretly introduce destructive heresies, even denying the sovereign Lord who bought them—bringing swift destruction on themselves. Many will follow their shameful ways and will bring the way of truth into disrepute. In their greed these teachers will exploit you with stories they have made up. Their condemnation has long been hanging over them, and their destruction has not been sleeping" (2 Peter 2:1–3).

As you already know, Martin Luther was excommunicated from the Catholic religious system because he saw the whole business of purgatory as a confidence trick and a cheat. Luther's very life was at stake. He would have been killed but for the intervention of Prince Frederick. Luther's story is well known.

In the authorized *Catechism of the Catholic Church,* which has been used throughout this book as the source of the doctrines of the Catholic religious system, we read:

> *The Eucharistic sacrifice* is also offered for *the faithful departed* who "have died in Christ but are *not yet wholly purified,*" so that they may be able to enter into the light and peace of Christ: [from this point, the text is a quote from St. Monica from this same source].
>
> Then, we pray . . . for the holy fathers and bishops who have fallen asleep [died], and in general for all who have fallen asleep before us, *in the belief that it is a great benefit to the souls on whose behalf the supplication is offered,* while the holy and tremendous Victim [Eucharistic sacrifice] is present. . . . *By offering to God our supplications for those who have fallen asleep*, if they have sinned, we . . .offer Christ sacrificed for the sins of all, and so render favorable, for them and for us, the God who loves man."[3]

(Italicization above and in the quote below by this author.)

One more quote from the *Catechism* will provide a slightly clearer picture of what purgatory is: "From the beginning the Church has honored the memory of the dead and offered prayers in suffrage for them, above all the Eucharistic sacrifice so that, thus purified, they may attain the beatific vision of God [meaning getting into heaven]. *The Church also commends almsgiving, indulgences, and works of penance undertaken on behalf of the dead.*"[4]

Those statements from the 1994 *Catechism* do not begin to reveal the workings of the system of purgatory. The system is hinted at through the words *Eucharist, almsgiving, indulgences,* and *works of penance*, but there is far more to it.

The reason for purgatory is that, according to Catholic doctrine, the popes, bishops, and priests can only forgive sins that are known about while the person is here on earth. After a Catholic dies, he/she is now faced with the sins that only God knows about; the sins God can see in a person that the person himself might not be aware of, or sins that had never been admitted to a priest.

Those sins have to be forgiven before the Catholic believer can move on into heaven. How will these sins be forgiven? The answer, of course, is in the doctrine of purgatory.

There were several subsystems associated with getting through and out of purgatory: indulgences, penance, relics, the treasury of merit, Masses for the dead, and individual prayers for the dead. The amount of religious attention a Catholic gives to indulgences, penance, relics, the treasury of merit, Masses, and prayers for the dead, will determine how long a Catholic will spend in purgatory.

The sale of indulgences was a significant means for the popes to acquire funds for their building projects and other adventures. To repeat, in 1517, Pope Leo X wanted to complete the building of St. Peter's Basilica in Rome, plus he had to pay off a large loan to a banking firm.

How would he get the money? The pope offered an indulgence to those (rich and poor) who would contribute. Of course, if there was a contribution, depending upon how much was given, a certain number of years in purgatory would be subtracted from what had been accumulated.

As you already know, it was Pope Leo's indulgence that stimulated Martin Luther to ignite the flame of the Protestant Reformation.

When a Catholic goes to a priest to confess sins and a penance is charged to the confessor, the priest can require a gift to the Catholic Church as a required payment to ensure forgiveness. A penance can include payment to the church for an indulgence that would reduce the time in purgatory.

Roland H. Bainton in his book, *Here I Stand: A Life of Martin Luther,* gives some examples of how relics were used to get time off in purgatory.

> Every relic of the saints in Halle, for example, was endowed by Pope Leo X with an indulgence for the reduction of purgatory by four thousand years. The greatest storehouse for such treasures was Rome. Here in a single crypt of St. Callistus, forty popes were buried and 76,000 martyrs. Rome had a piece of Moses' burning bush and three hundred particles of the Holy Innocents. Rome had the portrait of Christ on the napkin of St. Veronica. Rome had the chains of St. Paul and scissors with which Emperor Domitian clipped the hair of St. John. The walls of Rome near the Appian gate showed the white spots left by the stones which turned to snowballs when hurled by the mob against St. Peter before his time was come. A church in Rome had the crucifix which leaned over to talk to St. Brigitta. Another had a coin paid to Judas for betraying our Lord. Its value had greatly increased, for now it was able to confer an indulgence of fourteen hundred years.[5]

It wasn't just the common folk who were captivated by indulgences and relics. Frederick the Wise, the elector of Saxony, Luther's prince, was an avid collector of relics. (Italicization below by this author.)

The collection had as its nucleus a genuine thorn from the crown of Christ, certified to have pierced the Savior's brow. Frederick so built up the collection from this inherited treasure that the catalogue illustrated by Lucas Cranach in 1509 listed 5,005 particles, to which were attached indulgences calculated to reduce purgatory by 1,443 years. . . . By 1520 the collection had mounted to 19,013 holy bones. Those who viewed these relics *on the designated day and made the stipulated contributions* might receive from the pope indulgences for the reduction of purgatory, either for themselves or others, to the extent of 1,902,202 years and 270 days. These were the treasures made available on the day of All Saints [November 1].[6]

Eamon Duffy in his book, The *Stripping of the Altars*, cites two examples of the ridiculous notion of years off in purgatory.

The fifteenth century had seen the circulation of devotional woodcuts which the faithful were encouraged to meditate on, to kneel before, to kiss. These images often had indulgences attached to them, encouraging a devotion which might be mechanical or meditative, but at any rate not verbal. One typical image of Christ as the Man of Sorrows, surrounded by the Implements of the Passion—nails, scourges, lance, cross, vernicle and so on—carried the promise that "To them that before this ymage of pyte devoutly say fyve Pater noster fyve Aveys & a Crede pytously beholding these armes of Christ's passyon ar graunted 32,755 yeres of pardon."[7]

You may find it interesting that Pope Francis, the current pope, declared the time from November 1, 2015 to November 1, 2016 the Year of Mercy. Pope Francis also declared an indulgence for all Catholics, everywhere. That would, according to Catholic calculations, be about one billion people. What was the indulgence? It was to forgive all of the sins [past, present, and up to All Saints Day in 2016] of all of the one billion Catholics for a whole year. The Eugene, Oregon, *Register Guard* reported the Pope's declaration: "Speaking from the central balcony of St. Peter's Basilica, Francis issued a plenary indulgence for all Catholics in hopes of spreading the church's message of mercy in a world torn by war, poverty, and extremist attacks. An indulgence is an ancient church tradition related to the forgiveness of sins. . . . Francis said he hoped the plenary indulgence he issued for this, his Holy Year of Mercy, would encourage the faithful 'to welcome God's mercy in our lives, and be merciful with our brothers to make peace grow.'" [8]

It is clear from Pope Francis' indulgence, that forgiving Catholic's sins is still an active heresy in the Catholic religious system. In the article above, we aren't told what it cost each Catholic for Pope Francis' indulgence. According to Bainton's book in the passage quoted above, we read that there was a stipulated contribution as a regular feature of a pope granting an indulgence.

With Pope Francis' indulgence, we can assume that getting these earthly sins forgiven will significantly reduce the time in purgatory for all the one billion Catholics.

Perhaps the payoff will come when priests all over the world upon hearing confessions, will for the required penance, require a stipulated contribution for Rome.

Interestingly, Pope Francis issued his indulgence to correspond to the time frame of his Year of Mercy. It was to begin on November 1, which is All Saints Day, or sometimes known as the Day of the Dead. It so happens that the indulgence mentioned in Bainton's book also began on All Saints Day, an interesting coincidence.

Do you believe Pope Francis, or any other pope, can indulge (forgive) a Catholic's sins for some sort of contribution? Do you believe it is in the power of a so-called pope to forgive the sins of others? Do you believe that viewing supposed relics on a given day will buy a Catholic years off of purgatory? Can you believe that saying Masses (particularly the Eucharist) for the dead will get a Catholic friend or relative through purgatory quicker? Is there such a thing as purgatory? Is it ever mentioned in the Bible?

Not only is purgatory not mentioned anywhere in the Bible, the concept is a complete distortion of what happens when a true believer sins, or when that believer in Jesus the Christ dies.

According to the Bible, how and when are a person's sins forgiven?

When we sin, who is it that has a case against us? Who is it that needs to forgive? How is forgiveness achieved?

The psalmist, David in this case, had this to say about who was the offended when he deliberately committed adultery with Bathsheba and then had Bathsheba's husband killed. He knew against whom he had sinned, and he knew that he had an open door to go directly to God. He needed no human mediator. He knew where and from whom to get forgiveness. "Have mercy on me, O God, according to your unfailing love; according to your great compassion blot out my transgressions. Wash away all my iniquity and cleanse me from my sin. For I know my transgressions, and my sin is always before me. Against you, you only, have I sinned and done what is evil in your sight, so that you are proved right when you speak and justified when you judge" (Ps. 51:1–4).

When David committed adultery with Bathsheba and had Uriah killed, he hurt a lot of people, including his own family,

Bathsheba's family, and the nation of Israel. And, yet, his confession is directly to God. It was God whom he had offended. It was from God he needed satisfaction and cleansing. It was only God through whom he sought forgiveness.

Perhaps David sought forgiveness from the people he had sinned against, but there is no record of that happening.

In the New Testament, God has revealed to us that there is a mediator.

> Therefore, since we have a great high priest who has gone through the heavens, Jesus the Son of God, let us hold firmly to the faith we profess. For we do not have a high priest who is unable to sympathize with our weaknesses, but we have one who has been tempted in every way, just as we are—yet was without sin. Let us then approach the throne of grace with confidence, so that we may receive mercy and find grace to help us in our time of need (Heb. 4:14–16).

> If we confess our sins [to Jesus], he is faithful and just and will forgive us our sins and purify us from all unrighteousness (1 John 1:9).

> My dear children, I write this to you so that you will not sin. But if anybody does sin, we have one who speaks to the Father in our defense—Jesus Christ, the Righteous One. He is the atoning sacrifice for our sins, and not only for ours but also for the sins of the whole world (1 John 2:1–2).

Could it be clearer than that? We need no one but Jesus to go to with our sins.

Jesus made it very clear to a group of Jews that he could, and would forgive sins.

Jesus stepped into a boat, crossed over and came to his own town. Some men brought to him a paralytic, lying on a mat. When Jesus saw their faith, he said to the paralytic, "Take heart, son; your sins are forgiven." At this, some of the teachers of the law said to themselves, "This fellow is blaspheming!" Knowing their thoughts, Jesus said, "Why do you entertain evil thoughts in your hearts? Which is easier: to say, 'Your sins are forgiven,' or to say, 'Get up and walk'? But so that you may know that the Son of Man has authority on earth to forgive sins." Then he said to the paralytic, "Get up, take your mat and go home." And the man got up and went home. When the crowd saw this, they were filled with awe; and they praised God, who had given such authority to men (Matt. 9:1–8).

First of all, let's remember once again that there is no person on this earth who has not sinned. Let us remember, too, that one of these sinners goes around claiming that he has the authority from Jesus to forgive sins. This sinful man uses the appellation *pope*. He claims, too, that the bishops and priests who have completed Holy Orders under the rules of the Catholic religious system can also forgive sins. So, in the Catholic religious system there are popes, bishops, and priests who have the power and authority to forgive sins.

Remembering the story of the paralytic whom Jesus healed (Mark 2:1–12), we know that he told the paralytic, "Son, your sins are forgiven." The Jewish leaders who heard Jesus make that statement said, "He's blaspheming! Who can forgive sins but God alone?" Then Jesus said to them, "But that you may know that the Son of Man has authority on earth to forgive sins." And he healed the paralytic.

The unstated truth in the above story of the paralytic is that Jesus is God.

In Jesus' lifetime, he did many, many miraculous works all of which were signs that he was the Son of God and that he was authorized and worthy by his sinless life to forgive sins. John said, "Jesus did many other things as well. If every one of them were written down, I suppose that even the whole world would not have room for the books that would be written" (John 21:25).

We know from chapters 2 through 5 of this book that there is no such thing as popes, bishops (as defined by Catholicism), or priests. It is all a hoax, and in this discussion of forgiveness of sin, blasphemy. The Jewish leaders, when they accused Jesus of blasphemy because he said he forgave the paralytic's sins, were spot on. It would have been blasphemy if any other person on earth had made such a statement.

In the book of Hebrews, it is made very clear to us that there is only one source for the forgiveness of sins.

> In fact, the law requires that nearly everything be cleansed with blood, and without the shedding of blood there is no forgiveness. It was necessary, then, for the copies of the heavenly things to be purified with these sacrifices [referring back to the Old Testament requirements], but the heavenly things themselves with better sacrifices than these.
>
> For Christ did not enter a man-made sanctuary that was only a copy of the true one; he entered heaven itself, now to appear for us in God's presence. Nor did he enter heaven to offer himself again and again, the way the high priest enters the Most Holy Place every year with blood that is not his own. Then Christ would have had to suffer many times since the creation of the world. But now he has appeared once for all at the end of the ages to do away with sin by the sacrifice of himself. Just as man is destined to die once, and after that to face judgment, so Christ was sacrificed once to take away the sins of many people; and he will appear a

second time, not to bear sin, but to bring salvation to those who are waiting for him (Heb. 9:22–28).

Notice in the above, and it is said many times in various places but especially in the book of Hebrews, that "without the shedding of blood there is no forgiveness." And, of course, it was the blood of Christ shed while he was crucified on the cross. In reality, the blood of Christ represented the very life of Jesus the Christ that was given: "The life of a creature is in the blood," as we are told in the Old Testament (Lev. 17:11).

The only medium of exchange for sin is the blood of Jesus. No amount of man-made religious sounding rules, rites, and rituals can substitute for that blood. No amount of man-made penances, indulgences, or prayers can be used in exchange for sin—to gain forgiveness for sin.

I trust you are convinced that that part of the purgatory heresy—forgiveness of sins—has no justification in Scripture. It is all based upon Catholic tradition that overruled Scripture. In the Catholic mind, Tradition trumps Scripture.

There is one more aspect of purgatory that needs examination. What happens to the genuine believer in Jesus when they die? Is purgatory their destination? In other words, does purgatory even exist? Or, what is the future of believers after they die?

It is an unrealistic expectation to attempt to bring every portion of Scripture to bear upon this question. As has been the practice throughout this book, I can only provide, in this case, a selected portion of what the Bible says about death, resurrection, and going to heaven.

Jesus made it clear that when a person believes in him and accepts him as Savior and Lord, something dramatic occurs. It isn't necessarily a dramatic outward experience, but something changes within the very soul and spirit of the new believer. This inner experience will be different for everyone. The person who has lived a long life of sinful behavior will undoubtedly have a different experience than the person who grew up in a Christian home and sort of slides right into a personal commitment of belief in Christ, sometimes, even while still a child. It is, essentially, a transaction that takes place in the soul and spirit.

Following are some of the things that are said in the Scriptures about what happens when a person receives Jesus into their very being. The partial and selected quotes below are taken from John's gospel, chapter 3.

> Now there was a man of the Pharisees [a very religious man] named Nicodemus, a member of the Jewish ruling council. He came to Jesus at night and said, "Rabbi, we know you are a teacher who has come from God. For no one could perform the miraculous signs you are doing if God were not with him."
>
> In reply Jesus declared, "I tell you the truth, no one can see the kingdom of God unless he is born again."
>
> [Nicodemus commented], "Surely he cannot enter a second time into his mothers' womb to be born!"
>
> Jesus answered, "Flesh gives birth to flesh, but the Spirit gives birth to spirit. You should not be surprised at my saying, 'You must be born again . . . '"
>
> "How can this be?" Nicodemus asked.
>
> [Jesus replied,] "For God so loved the world that he gave his one and only Son, that whoever believes in him shall not perish but have eternal life. For God did not send his Son into the world to condemn the world, but to save the world through him. Whoever believes in him is not condemned, but whoever does not believe stands condemned already because he has not believed in the name of God's one and only Son" (John 3:1–18).

When Jesus responded to Nicodemus, he answered the question about how one is born again by putting his answer in terms of believing in the Son of God, himself. However, the apostle Paul gives us some insight into what it means to be born again. (Italicization by this author.)

> Therefore, if anyone is *in Christ*, he is *a new creation*; the old has gone, the new has come! (2 Cor. 5:17)

> For we are God's workmanship, *created in Christ Jesus* to do good works, which God prepared in advance for us to do (Eph. 2:10).

> You were taught, with regard to your former way of life, to put off your old self, which is being corrupted by its deceitful desires; to be made new in the attitude of your minds; and to put on the new self, *created to be like God in true righteousness and holiness* (Eph. 4:22–24).

When a person believes in Jesus as Savior and Lord and openly confesses that belief, he is a new creation. This is what Jesus was introducing to Nicodemus when he told him that he must be born again.

Now, at that moment of belief, something with eternal consequences also occurs to the newly created believer. Jesus said this: "I tell you the truth, whoever hears my word and believes him who sent me has eternal life and will not be condemned; he has [already] crossed from death to life" (John 5:24).

The new believer already has eternal life. He/she has crossed from death to [eternal] life. "Being strengthened with all power according to his glorious might so that you may have great endurance and patience, and joyfully giving thanks to the Father, who has qualified you to share in the inheritance of the saints in the kingdom of light. For he has rescued us from the dominion of darkness and brought us into the kingdom of the Son he loves, in whom we have [already possess] redemption, the forgiveness of sins" (Col. 1:11–14).

Regarding the phrase *will not be condemned* in John 5:24, Paul later said this: "Therefore, there is now no condemnation for those who are *in Christ Jesus*, because through Christ Jesus the law of the Spirit of life set me free from the law of sin and death (Rom. 8:1–2). (Italicization by this author.)

The little word *in* that begins the phrase *in Christ Jesus*, is a very significant word. *Strong's Exhaustive Concordance of the Bible* says this little word means, "denoting (fixed) *position* (in place, time or state), . . . i.e. a relation of *rest*."[9]

Therefore, it is necessary to ask, "Where is this *place*, and what is the *time*, and what *state* is meant? The apostle Paul helps us answer these questions. "Since, then, you have been raised with Christ, set your hearts on things above, where Christ is seated at the right hand of God. Set your minds on things above, not on earthly things. For you died, and your life is now hidden with Christ in God. When Christ, who is your life, appears, then you also will appear with him in glory" (Col. 3:1–4).

The state, of course, is that the believer is in Christ. The place is in Christ in heaven (already there). Believers are seated with Christ at the right hand of God. The time when all this happened is when the believer was raised with Christ [resurrected with Christ]. And this is all sealed by the Father: "For you died, and your life is now hidden with Christ in God."

What does it mean for a believer to be hidden with Christ in God? We can look to Strong's Concordance again. It means to "*conceal* by covering; to hide; and to keep secret."[10]

And what is the *covering*? Believers are covered within the folds of the righteousness of Christ. [Abraham was] "fully persuaded that God had power to do what he had promised. This is why 'it was credited to him as righteousness.' The words 'it was credited to him' were written not for him alone, but also for us, to whom God will credit righteousness—for us who believe in him who raised Jesus our Lord from the dead. He was delivered over to death for our sins and was raised to life for our justification" (Rom. 4:21–23).

In summary, from the beginning of this book, I have tried to dismantle the fundamental beliefs (pillars) upon which the Catholic religious system is based. I trust you imagined, as we went along, the cracking, crumbling, and the impending crash of those pillars.

The pillars of Catholicism were examined throughout chapters 2 through 11. Three pillars were personalized in Peter, the popes, and Mary. The remaining four pillars were associated with the sacramental system: tradition, water baptism, the Eucharist, and purgatory.

My purpose, relating to the book as a whole, was to do what the apostle Paul said we should do with aberrant beliefs. "For though we live in the world, we do not wage war as the world does. The weapons we fight with are not the weapons of the world. On the contrary, they have divine power to demolish strongholds. We demolish arguments and every pretension that sets itself up against the knowledge of God, and we take captive every thought to make it obedient to Christ" (2 Cor. 10:3–5).

What are the weapons with which we demolish strongholds? The only tried and true weapon we have is that of the Scriptures. I have used the Scriptures extensively and effectively, I trust, to implode the structure of the Catholic religious system.

I have not mentioned many personal names in this book, and I avoided accusing, as best I could, any individual of evil or evil motives.

Only God knows exactly who is a Christian and those who are not. I'm sure there are Catholics who truly believe in and have received Jesus as their Savior and Lord. But I am sure that there are millions of confessing Catholics who will go straight to hell when they die.

As you now know, there is no such place as purgatory; a kind of halfway house where one can get fixed up so that they will eventually make it into heaven. "Just as man is destined to die once, and after that to face judgment" (Heb. 9:27) is a sobering statement in Scripture. There is no halfway house.

Whatever happened to Jesus? That was the fundamental question asked in the title of this book. As we went along, it became obvious, and it was noted in the text, that we must also ask, whatever happened to the Holy Spirit?

You must have noticed as you read, that the Catholic religious system effectively devoured Jesus and the Holy Spirit. They buried Jesus, the Holy Spirit, and the Scriptures underneath a religious system that elevated people and dogmas in their place.

In effect the Catholics buried Jesus, the Holy Spirit, and the Scriptures by piling on top of these two persons of the Trinity, and upon their inspired Word, the doctrines of demons, as Paul defined them. And what was the original source of these doctrines of demons? "Why is my language not clear to you? Because you are unable to hear what I say. You belong to your father, the devil, and you want to carry out your father's desire. He was a murderer from the beginning, not holding to the truth, for there is no truth in him. When he lies, he speaks his native language, for he is a liar and the father of lies. Yet because I tell you the truth you do not believe me" (John 8:43–45).

I do hope this book will help some who are seeking Christ to find him. I also hope it will be used in the lives of many Catholics to understand the evil nature of their religious system and to abandon that system.

One purpose of this book was to provide a resource by which anyone could rightly judge Catholicism and be able to share this resource with people they meet who need to know the truth about Catholicism.

So, to God be the glory for whatever benefit this work might have in the life of anyone who reads it.

One final word from Scripture: "Therefore Jesus said again, 'I tell you the truth, I am the gate for the sheep. All who ever came before me were thieves and robbers, but the sheep did not listen to them. I am the gate; whoever enters through me will be saved. He will come in and go out, and find pasture. The thief comes only to steal and kill and destroy; I have come that they may have life, and have it to the full'" (John 10:7–10).

If you are a Catholic, please consider carefully what has been revealed in this chapter. Have you bought into the greatest scam ever known on the face of this earth?

A friend of mine, while discussing religion with a Catholic acquaintance of his, asked the man if he was counting on the Catholic Church to get him into heaven? The acquaintance answered, "They better get me in; I've given them enough money."

That Catholic man is a victim of the most insidious scam every imagined.

Finally, let us think back on the seven pillars of the Catholic religious system: Peter, the popes, Mary, tradition, water baptism, the Eucharist, and purgatory. Scripture truths were packed around each of these pillars.

It is time to activate the implosion. Will you push the plunger? If not you, I will.

I trust you can by a little imagination see the whole structure of the Catholic religious system plunging in a cloud of diabolical dust and debris.

Now, I don't want to leave the reader with such a negative thought. That is why I wrote chapter 12. Chapter 12 is the story of my journey from unbelief to the moment when I asked Jesus to come into my life and some of what happened as a result.

And, as I mentioned in the introduction to this book, the background for ever getting involved in writing this book had to do with my desire to find my Christian roots. So, in chapter 12, I also tell where I found those roots.

I pray my personal story will point the reader to Jesus and to Jesus only.

CHAPTER 12

ONE MAN'S JOURNEY

BEFORE I TELL my story, it's important to say that in my fifty-eight years of Christian life, I have heard many people tell stories of how Jesus came into their lives. And the story is always different. So when I tell my story here, please remember that the circumstances I will relate are not the norm. I guess it is like our fingerprints; there are no two hands exactly alike.

"Therefore, if anyone is in Christ, he is a new creation; the old has gone, the new has come!" (2 Cor. 5:17). There could be no more fitting words to begin the story of how Jesus came into my life than those words from the apostle Paul. Let me tell you how it began; how I became a "new creation."

I was a senior in high school. It was the end of a school day. I was walking home from basketball practice. On Washington Street in the small farming town of Gooding, Idaho, there is a place where the roots of a huge elm tree had undermined the sidewalk. You know how it is, the sidewalk had buckled and one had to walk up over the undermining roots. Just as I stepped over the large crack in the concrete, a voice spoke to me (it must have been God).

The words were, "Do you believe in God?"

For some reason beyond my understanding, I wasn't surprised, startled, or suspicious. However, I was surprised at my response. I said, "Yes." The reason I was surprised at my response was that I did not remember ever in my life even thinking if there was a God. How strange it seemed as I reflected on the fact that I had said, "Yes."

You see, I was raised in a family where God was never talked about, unless there was some negative connotation or some swearing. By the time I was a senior in high school, I was very good at the swearing business. I used Jesus' name and God's name frequently in angry and expletive-filled statements directed at others or directed at circumstances and events I didn't like.

I cannot remember ever seeing a Bible in our home. As far as I remember, up to and through my high school years, I had never had a Bible in my hands.

So, that evening on that broken sidewalk, the way I responded was a mystery to me.

A few weeks after that sidewalk event and on a Saturday morning, my sister had turned on the radio to a channel of country-western music. She had left the house without turning the radio off.

When I came in from outdoors, it was no longer country-western music, but a country-western preacher. I had no intention of listening. I went to turn the radio off, but just as I twisted the dial to off, the preacher said, "You can know God."

That night, as I lay in bed, the statement, "You can know God" kept resonating in my mind. The preacher's words meant to me that the God I had said (that afternoon on the broken sidewalk) I believed in was a God I could know.

Oh, I thought, could I really know God? If a person could actually know God, well, that would be the best thing that could ever happen. That would be the best thing that could ever happen to me. I never forgot that idea, that possibility. But how? I had turned off the radio.

Parenthetically, when I was ten years old, there was an event, the significance of which I wasn't to realize until some years later.

My mom and dad had to go to another city to interview for jobs. They left me at Aunt Esther's for a couple of days. While I was there, Aunt Viola came for coffee one morning. They were in the kitchen, and I was sitting in the living room reading a comic book. I heard some of their conversation. Aunt Viola was telling Aunt Esther about Jesus.

Apparently, Viola said to Esther, something like this: "You need to ask Jesus to come into your life." The only thing I remembered from that whole conversation was Esther's response. She said, "I'm not going to now, but if I ever do, I'll go all the way."

It was those words, "If I ever do, I'll go all the way," that were seared into my subconscious. I didn't know those words were there until some years later.

Now back to the main story line.

I heard no more (after the radio preacher) about God, or from God, for several months.

I graduated from high school and enrolled at a junior college. I had a football scholarship and dreamed of being a civil engineer. I wanted to build roads and bridges.

It didn't take long for my dream world of football player and engineer to unravel. I don't know all the reasons, but football (a sport I loved—I was captain of the football team in high school) suddenly lost its appeal. And in the classroom, it became apparent that I was not cut out to be an engineer.

I quit school and joined the navy. As we processed through boot camp, the last item we were given to load into our sea bags was a New Testament provided by a group called the Gideons. Here, now, was the first Bible I had ever had in my hands. However, at that point, it didn't mean anything to me.

After boot camp, I was sent to Imperial Beach, California, for further training. Imperial Beach is very close to Tijuana, Mexico. That seemed good to me as I could pursue the fulfillment of desires that, even though unhealthy and ungodly, had long been part of my lifestyle.

One night, arriving back in the barracks after a visit to Tijuana, for the first time in my life, I experienced a strong sense of guilt and shame. After all of the other nights, why that night?

What do you do with guilt and shame? I had no idea this is what is called in the Bible a conviction of sin. As I stood by my bunk, the conviction of my sinful life just wouldn't go away.

I remembered the New Testament. It was on a shelf in my locker. I started reading. It was absolutely meaningless to me. But, on the back flyleaf, there was a place to sign your name and put the date if you wanted to be "saved." I signed and marked the date.

The only thing in my life that changed was the growing feeling of an absolute sense of emptiness in my life. This sense of emptiness grew as I was transferred to Hawaii and later to the Philippines. I came to the point of actually saying to myself one night, "I don't care if I live or die."

Actually, as the months rolled on, another feeling began to surge up into my consciousness. It was the feeling that I didn't really want to die. In fact, I was afraid to die. I knew if there was a God who was holy, righteous, and just, and if there was a place called hell, God would have no option but to send me there. I was clear, crystal clear, on where I would go.

I didn't want to go to hell, whatever that meant.

Let me say at this time that all of this personal experience was preparing me for inviting Jesus into my life. I just didn't know it at the time.

While in the Philippines, on the job one day, the supervisor (Chief Petty Officer, Ralph) of my duty station came up to me and said, "Paul, my wife and I have just become Christians, and we are starting a Bible study this Friday night at our home. We would like you to come."

I was annoyed at his invitation. It embarrassed me because I knew some of the other men had heard what was said. My reply was less than kind.

I said, with as much vitriol as I could, "Why are you asking me?"

He said, "We don't know anyone that needs it more than you do!" How did he know that?

Interestingly, for Christmas that year, my mother had sent me a Bible. It was one of those black Bibles with a zipper. It said *Holy Bible* on the front. "It must be the real thing," I thought. Also, in the second half of that book, there was a lot of red writing. I wondered what that red writing was for. As you might know, in that translation of the Bible, Jesus' words were printed in red.

Well, Friday night was coming; I had a new Bible so, I thought, maybe I'll go to the Bible study. However, an academy award-winning movie was going to be shown on the base that Friday night. I really wanted to see *The Gunfight at OK Corral.* I went to the movie.

While viewing the beginning of the movie, it seemed to me to be the most ridiculous movie I had ever seen. "What a loser," I said to myself. I left the movie, went back to the barracks for my new Bible, and went to the Bible study.

When I arrived, there were about twelve people sitting around the living room. The study had already begun.

As I sat down, obviously not knowing what to do, Ralph took my Bible and opened to what I learned later was the book of Daniel. I had no idea there was even a book called Daniel. That is how ignorant I was.

But as the group discussed the text before them that evening, one thing became clear to me: these people all seemed to know God, and I didn't. But I also thought of that country-western preacher and his words, "You can know God." Ever since hearing those words, I had wanted to know God. Here at the Bible study were some people who might tell me how.

When the study ended, I stayed until everyone had left. I said to Ralph, "You all seem to know God, how could I get to know God?"

Ralph took my Bible once again and opened it, not to the book of Daniel this time, but to a place in the New Testament where there was some of that red writing.

Later, I would know that it was the book of the gospel of John, and that it was the third chapter.

Ralph pointed to some of that red writing and said, "Here, read this." So, I read the very well-known text John 3:16. It said, "For God so loved the world that he gave his one and only Son, that whoever believes in him shall not perish but have eternal life."

Those words, "Shall not perish" caught my attention. Shall not go to hell was what those words meant to me. There was, then, a possibility of being saved.

But what was the condition? It was simply, "whoever believes in him." Obviously, that meant to believe in Jesus. Well, if you want to do that, how do you do it? That is what I asked Ralph.

He told me that I had to pray and ask Jesus to come into my life and be my Savior. "What do you pray?" I asked. I had never prayed before. I didn't know what to say to Jesus.

I was given a kind of short, model prayer. I was told to pray those words and Jesus would come into my heart. I bowed my head, but I found I didn't say those words. The following, is what I prayed: "Jesus, I don't know who you are, but if you can save me and keep me from going to hell, I want you to come into my life."

As I prayed those words, a memory surfaced. It was the words my Aunt Esther had said those several years past: "If I ever do, I'll go all the way." Those words became the very motive in my own mind; "I'm going all the way." I had the sense that this was to be total commitment on my part.

It was not a religious, sentimental, or emotional experience. There were no outward indicators that anything had happened: no bells and whistles. I didn't know anything had happened until I went back to the barracks.

At the end of the barracks was a lounge where it was comfortable to sit. When I walked in, two of my friends were sitting there. They were wondering where I was.

One of them asked me, "Where have you been?" But the other one said, "You look different. What has happened to you?"

I often wondered what it was that caused my friend to say, "You look different." I didn't feel any different at that moment. What did he see? The only answer I've ever been able to come up with is that he saw something different in my face. He was used to seeing such expressions as anger, frustration, criticism, hostility, and emptiness on my countenance. What was he seeing now?

I do know this: my life began to change. Jesus had come into my life. I was a new creation. Past habits and desires started dropping off quickly. I don't mean that I became some kind of religious holy person, but it is true I became a different person. And some of that difference showed up overnight.

For example, I had a habitually foul mouth. I used the names *Jesus* and *Jesus Christ* profusely as curses. It was an amazing thing to me, and I'm sure to those who knew me, that profanity ceased to be a part of my conversation instantly. It's always been a marvel to me how that aspect of my life disappeared so quickly. I guess it seems obvious and logical that it would. After all, it was Jesus who saved me and who had come into my life; I mean right into my very being.

There were other things that changed, but I have said enough. However, I do want to tell you about one more aspect of my life that was turned upside down.

I mentioned earlier that I had dropped out of college because my dreams about what I would do had come crashing down. I had lost any sense of purpose in life. You know, the age-old questions: Why am I here? What do I have to live for? The navy certainly didn't provide answers to those questions, at least, for me.

A couple of months later I learned that two missionaries who were translating the Bible into an unwritten language there in the Philippines had friends in that Friday night Bible study group and had been invited to share about their work. When the missionaries told us that the ethnic group for whom they were translating the Bible was just one of thousands of groups of people all around the world without the Bible in their language, well, I was immediately on alert.

That night after the meeting, I went back to the barracks and before going to bed, got down on my knees and prayed. I asked God to give me the opportunity to help get the Bible translated for all those other groups of people, which, by the way, turned out to be about 2,000 different groups.

The thought that was predominant in my mind before I prayed was that if these groups of people never had the Bible in their own language, they might never hear about Jesus dying for them. My thoughts went back to the night Jesus came into my life. Specifically, I thought of when the leader took my Bible out of my hands and opened it to John 3:16. His words were, "Here read this." On my knees, what came to my mind was that for all those groups of people without the Bible, if someone in those groups wanted to know God, no one could say to them, "Here read this." No one could point to John 3:16 in their language. It didn't exist. It wouldn't exist unless someone learned their spoken language, created a written form of their language, and translated the Bible into their language.

God answered that prayer: "Lord, give me the opportunity to help!" My wife and I were eventually provided the opportunity to spend forty years of our lives serving with a Bible translation organization. Not only did Jesus come into my life, but he gave me a purpose for living that I couldn't have imagined.

Dear reader, how would you describe your relationship to Jesus? Is Christ in you? Have you ever asked him to come into your life? Have you admitted to yourself that you are a sinner? Have you ever confessed this to God—to Jesus? Are you, in some way, trying to buy your way into heaven like the media man I mentioned above?

Please note that if you thought you could buy your way into heaven, you need to understand that you don't have anything to offer God that is equal to the blood of Jesus Christ. "Without the shedding of blood there is no remission of sin" (Heb. 9:22).

Do you want to be saved? Here is what Jesus has to say to you: "So be earnest, and repent. Here I am! I stand at the door [of your soul] and knock. If anyone hears my voice and opens the door, I will come in and eat with him, and he with me" (Rev. 3:19–20).

Do you know what it means that Jesus will eat with you? It means he will come into your very being and begin an eternal fellowship with you. He will be your companion forever and ever. But, you have to open the door.

"Whoever believes in the Son has eternal life, but whoever rejects the Son will not see life, for God's wrath remains on him" (John 3:36).

And, if you do open the door, this is what Jesus promises: "I tell you the truth, whoever hears my word and believes him who sent me has eternal life and will not be condemned; he has crossed over from death to life" (John 5:24).

So, there it is; your choice. Just pray a simple prayer like this: Jesus, I want to be saved, and I want you to come into my life. Right now I am opening the door of my very soul and life to you. I want you to come in.

Then, pick up a Bible and start reading the Gospel of John. Start praying for a church to attend. Find a church that preaches and teaches the gospel you've just been reading about. It is important that you begin reading in the Bible. When Jesus said that he would, "come in and eat," the food on the table that you will partake of as you fellowship with Jesus will be the Word of God: the Scriptures.

Peter put it this way, "Like newborn babies, crave pure spiritual milk, so that by it you may grow up in your salvation, now that you have tasted that the Lord is good" (1 Pet. 2:2).

If you know anyone whom you believe is a genuine Christian, let them know what you've just done. Tell your friends.

God bless you!

Now, I must go on to finish my story. In the Introduction, I also said I would tell the reader where I found my Christian roots. You see, that is what I was looking for when I started the research that turned out to inspire this particular book.

I found there were three streams of thought that flowed out of three different expressions of Christianity. All three expressions were stimulated by, and came from reading about, particular movements from within what we know as the Protestant Reformation: the Puritans, the Pilgrims, and the Pietists.

The Puritans were called by that appellation not because they were more moral than anyone else, but because they believed there was pure doctrine, and it wasn't being taught in either the Catholic or the Anglican religious systems.

George F. Willison in his book, *Saints and Strangers* tells about the Puritans and what they stood for.

> True radicals in seeking the root of things, they dug into Scripture to discover just where "disorder" had first crept in. The more they dug and explored, the less warrant could they find for a great deal of current belief and observance. The originally simple Christian faith had been corrupted, they declared, by time and "human invention." The obvious need of the hour was to restore it to its "ancient purity" . . . . Such views upset the orthodox, and in 1565 Archbishop Parker denounced those who advanced them as "these precise men." The phrase was graphic and seemed to fit, and the reformers were soon known as the Precisians, somewhat

later as the Puritans–so named, it should be observed, not for their moral code but for their theological doctrine.[1]

Therein lies one of my roots: Precisianists. In this book, I have tried to be as precise as I could be in revealing the errors of the Catholics and in quoting Scripture and giving the meaning of that Scripture. In this sense, I am to the best of my ability, a Precisianist, a Puritan.

There is another group who came out of the Protestant Reformation who were titled the Pilgrims. We Americans know all about them as they were some of the first settlers of our country. What drove them out of England, to Holland, and subsequently to America?

They were driven by this firm conviction: no one, not even the King or Queen of England, had the right to tell them who would be the pastors of their churches and to tell them how to worship the Lord their God.

The Pilgrims were called Separatists by some. They desired to separate from the Anglican Church and its top-down base of authority. In this, they were different from the Puritans. Willison explains, "Under increasing pressure many of the Puritans, especially those who were more comfortably situated in life, began to give way and resign themselves to at least a nominal conformity, fearing to jeopardize their personal safety, their bread and butter, even their creature comforts. But those of greater faith and courage were determined to go on. If there was no place for them in the church [the Church of England], they would withdraw and establish one of their own in which they might worship as they pleased. Come what might, they would defy the bishops, even the Queen."[2]

I, too, strongly believe that no person outside of a local congregation should have any absolute authority over that congregation. I believe with the Pilgrims, that each congregation should choose its pastor and other leaders, and that group of Christians should determine their bylaws and methods of worship. So, in this essential belief of the Pilgrims, I found another one of my roots.

Lastly, I found myself identifying with a much lesser known spin off of the Protestant Reformation called the Pietists. Pietism could be found in several different offshoots of the Protestant Reformation, but the term *evangelical* can serve as an umbrella term. Diarmaid MacCulloch defines it this way, "Like the Pietists and Moravians, English Evangelicals sought to create a religion of the heart and of direct personal relationship with Jesus Christ."[3]

It isn't that the Puritans and the Pilgrims didn't have this same thought that Pietists had, it's just that the Pietists made it a strong, insistent element of what it meant to be a Christian.

For the Pietist, unless one had a personal testimony of belief in and commitment to Jesus as both Lord and Savior (this is my interpretation of their emphasis), that person could not be recognized as a Christian. A continuing personal relationship with Jesus was also an element of the Pietist's beliefs.

So, in the Pietists, is where I found another essential element of my Christianity.

In my presentation of the Puritans, Pilgrims, and Pietists, there was no intent on my part to represent all that either of these groups believed. As I've tried to explain, there were certain special aspects of their beliefs that I strongly relate to: my roots, if you will.

In reading this chapter, you've become acquainted with this author in a way that most authors do not provide to the reader. I felt strongly that you should know exactly who wrote this book: *Peter, the Popes, and Mary: Whatever Happened to Jesus?*

I do hope that, by the grace of God, all that is contained in this book will pass the test of time and the test of truth over error.

> "And this is the testimony: God has given us eternal life, and this life is in his Son. He who as the Son has life; he who does not have the Son of God does not have life" (1 John 5:11–12).

> "Here I am! I stand at the door and knock. If anyone hears my voice and opens the door, I will come in and eat with him [or her], and he with me" (Rev. 3:20).

If you do not remember anything other than this absolute truth, "Christ in you, the hope of glory," perhaps this work will have served its best purpose.

BIBLIOGRAPHY

Ayer, Jr., PhD, Joseph Cullen. *A Source Book for Ancient Church History*. New York, NY: Charles Scribner's Sons, 1941.

Bainton, Roland H. *Here I Stand: A Life of Martin Luther*. Nashville, TN: Abingdon-Cokesbury Press, 1950.

Cheetham, Nicolas. *Keepers of the Keys*. New York, NY: Charles Scribner's Sons, 1983.

Curran, Bob. *Unholy Popes: Outrageous but True Stories of Papal Misbehavior*. New York, NY: Fall River Press, 2010.

Douglas, J.D., and Tenney, Merrill C. *NIV Compact Dictionary of the Bible*. Grand Rapids, MI: Zondervan Publishing House, 1989.

Doyle, Mary K. *Grieving with Mary; Finding Comfort and Healing in the Devotion to the Mother of God*. Skokie, IL: ACTA Publications, 2009.

Duffy, Eamon. *The Stripping of the Altars; Traditional Religion in England, 1400–1580*. New Haven and London: Yale University Press, 1992.

Durant, Will. *The Reformation: A History of European Civilization from Wycliffe to Calvin: 1300–1564.* New York, NY: MJF Books, 1985.

Garrigou-Lagrange, Reginald. *Reality: A Synthesis of Thomistic Thought.* St. Louis, MO: B. Herder Book Company, 1950.

Jamieson, Robert, Fausset, A.R. and Brown, David. *A Commentary: Critical, Experimental, and Practical of the Old and New Testaments: Volume Three, Part Three.* Grand Rapids, MI: William B. Eerdmans Publishing Company, no date.

Kidd, B.J. *The Counter-Reformation: 1550–1600.* London: Society for Promoting Christian Knowledge: A Publication of the Literature Association of the Church Union, 1937.

Libreria Editrice Vaticana. *Catechism of the Catholic Church.* New Hope, KY: Urbi et Orbi Communications, 1994.

MacCulloch, Diarmaid. *The Reformation.* New York, NY: Penguin Books, 2005.

—— *Christianity: The First Three Thousand Years.* New York, NY: Penguin Books, 2011.

Robertson, Archibald Thomas. *Word Pictures in the New Testament.* Grand Rapids, MI: Baker Book House, 1931.

Strong, James. *Strong's Exhaustive Concordance of the Bible.* Peabody, MA: Hendrickson Publishers, no date.

Vine, W.E. *An Expository Dictionary of New Testament Words: with their Precise Meanings for English Readers.* Old Tappan, NJ: Fleming H. Revell Company, 1966.

Walker, Williston. *A History of the Christian Church.* New York, NY: Charles Scribner's Sons, 1946.

Willison, George F. *Saints and Strangers.* New York, NY: Reynal & Hitchcock, 1945.

FURTHER SUGGESTED READING

Armstrong, Karen. *Holy War: The Crusades and Their Impact on Today's World.* New York, NY: Anchor Books, 2001.

Barron, Robert. *Bridging the Great Divide: Musings of a Post-Liberal, Post-Conservative Evangelical Catholic.* New York, NY: Rowan & Littlefield Publishers, Inc., 2004.

Bergendoff, Conrad. *The Church of the Lutheran Reformation: A Historical Survey of Lutheranism.* Saint Louis, MO: Concordia Publishing House, 1967.

Bettenson, Henry. *Documents of the Christian Church.* New York, NY: Oxford University Press, 1947.

Bradford, Ernie. *The Great Betrayal: Constantinople 1204.* New York, NY: White Lion Publishers Limited, 1967.

Brog, David. *In Defense of Faith: The Judeo-Christian Idea and the Struggle for Humanity.* New York, NY: Encounter Books, 2010.

Cahill, Thomas. *Mysteries of the Middle Ages: The rise of Feminism, Science, and Art from the Cults of Catholic Europe.* New York, NY: Doubleday, 2006.

Carroll, James. *Practicing Catholic.* New York, NY: Mariner Books, 2009.

Duggan, Alfred. *The Story of the Crusades.* New York, NY: Image Books, 1966.

Goguel, Maurice. *The Birth of Christianity.* London, England: George Allen and Unwin Ltd., 1953.

Haller, William. *The Rise of Puritanism.* London, England: Harper Torchbook, 1957.

Harnack, Adolf. *Outlines of the History of Dogma.* Boston, MA: Beacon Press, 1957.

Huizinga, Johan. *Erasmus and the Age of Reformation.* London, England: Harper Torchbook, 1957.

Martin, Malachi. *The Decline and Fall of the Roman Church.* New York, NY: G.P. Putnam's Sons, 1981.

McCarthy, Timothy G. *The Catholic Tradition: Before and After Vatican II, 1878–1993.* Chicago, IL: Loyola University Press, 1994.

Oberman, Heiko Augustinus. *Forerunners of the Reformation.* Philadelphia, PA: Fortress Press, 1981.

Pelikan, Jaroslav. *The Excellent Empire: The Fall of Rome and the Triumph of the Church.* San Francisco, CA: Harper and Row Publishers, 1971.

——*The Christian Tradition: A History of the Development of Doctrine.* Chicago, IL: The University of Chicago Press, 1975.

Scott, Ernest Findlay. *The Literature of the New Testament.* New York: Columbia University Press, 1945.

Yallop, David. *The Power and the Glory: Inside the Dark Heart of John Paul II's Vatican*. New York, NY: Carrol and Graf Publishers, 2007.

NOTES

Chapter 2 Peter as Presented in the New Testament
    1. Nicolas Cheetham, *Keepers of the Keys,* (New York, NY: Charles Scribner's Sons, 1983), 4.

Chapter 3 Was Peter the First Bishop of Rome?
    1. Ibid.
    2. Ibid.
    3. "Clements Writings," accessed September 15, 2015, www.earlychurchwritings.com/1clement.html.
    4. Cheetham, *Keepers of the Keys*, 4.
    5. Diarmaid MacCulloch, *Christianity: The First Three Thousand Years,* (New York, NY: Penguin Books Ltd., 2011), 135.
    6. Cheetham, *Keepers of the Keys*, 8.
    7. Ibid.
    8. Bob Curran, *Unholy Popes,* (New York, NY: Fall River Press, 2010), 8.

Chapter 4 The Rock, the Keys, and the Reality

1. James Strong, *Strong's Exhaustive Concordance of the Bible,* (Peabody, MA: Hendrickson Publishers, no date), found in Greek Dictionary of the New Testament section, 61, #4350.
2. J.D. Douglas & Merrill C. Tenney, *NIV Compact Dictionary of the Bible* (Grand Rapids, MI: Zondervan Publishing House, 1989), 172, "Eliakim."
3. Ibid., 330, "Key."

Chapter 5 The Dubious History of Popery

1. Joseph Cullen Ayer, Jr. PhD, *A Source Book for Ancient Church History,* (New York, NY: Charles Scribner's Sons, 1941), viii.
2. Clement's letter, accessed October 13, 2015, www.ewtn.com/library/patristc/anf1-1htm.
3. Cheetham, *Keepers of the Keys,* 9.
4. J. D. Douglas & Merrill C. Tenney, *NIV Compact Dictionary of the Bible,* 93, "Bishop."
5. Archibald Thomas Robertson AM, DD, LL, D, Litt. D., *Word Pictures in the New Testament,* (Grand Rapids, MI: Baker Book House, 1931), Vol. iv:, 572.
6. W. E. Vine, M.A., *An Expository Dictionary of New Testament Words,* (Old Tappan, NJ: Fleming H. Revell Company, 1966), 128, "Bishop."
7. Williston Walker, *A History of the Christian Church,* (New York, NY: Charles Scribner's Sons, 1946),48.
8. Vine, *An Expository Dictionary of New Testament Words,* 74–75.
9. Robertson, *Word Pictures in the New Testament,* 420.
10. Will Durant, *The Reformation* (New York, NY: MJF Books, 1985), 6.

11. Ibid.
12. Ibid., 7.
13. Ibid., 11.
14. Ibid., 13.

Chapter 6 Mary, the Temporary Mother of Jesus: the Son of Man
  1. Libreria Editrice Vaticana, *Catechism of the Catholic Church,* (New Hope, KY: URBI ET ORBI, 1994), 252.
  2. Ibid., 254.
  3. Ibid.
  4. Ibid.
  5. Ibid., 253.
  6. Mary K. Doyle, *Grieving with Mary,* (Skokie, IL: ACTA Publications, 2009), 32.
  7. Ibid., 86.
  8. Ibid., 77.
  9. Rev. Reginald Garrigou-Lagrange, O.P., *Reality: A Synthesis of Thomistic Thought,* (St. Louis, MO & London, WC: B. Herder Book Co., 1950), 242–243.

Chapter 7 An Introduction to the Sacramental System
  1. Cheetham, *Keepers of the Keys.*, 4.
  2. Ibid.
  3. B. J. Kidd, D.D., *The Counter-Reformation* (London, England: Society for Promoting Christian Knowledge, 1937), 53–113.
  4. Ibid.
  5. Ibid. 59.
  6. Ibid.
  7. Ibid.

8. Ibid., 60.
9. Ibid.
10. Ibid.
11. Libreria Editrice Vaticana, *Catechism of the Catholic Church*, 3.
12. Ibid., 5.
13. Ibid., 6.
14. Ibid., 26, #82.
15. Ibid., 27, #86.
16. Ibid., 27, #85.

Chapter 8 The Seven Sacraments
1. Libreria Editrice Vaticana, *Catechism of the Catholic Church*, 289, #1113.
2. Ibid., 282, #1086.
3. Ibid., 282–283, #1087.
4. Ibid., 289, #1116.
5. Ibid., 292, #1129.
6. Ibid., 293, #1131.

Chapter 9 Baptism of the Holy Spirit and Water Baptism
1. Libreria Editrice Vaticana, *Catechism of the Catholic Church,* 312, #1213.
2. Ibid., 323, #1271.
3. Ibid., 324, #1272.
4. Ibid., 324, #1277.
5. Ibid., 325, #1281.
6. Ibid., 325, #1278.
7. Ibid., 325, #1280.
8. Ibid., 323, #1271.
9. Robertson, *Word Pictures in the New Testament*, 493.

10. Robert Jamieson, A.R. Fausset, and David Brown, *A Commentary: Critical, Experimental, and Practical,* (Grand Rapids, MI: William B. Eerdmans Publishing Company), Vol. Three, 447.

Chapter 10 The Eucharist
1. Libreria Editrice Vaticana, *Catechism of the Catholic Church,* 289, #1114.
2. Ibid., 335, #1330.
3. Ibid., 341, #1353.
4. Ibid., 341, #1353.
5. Ibid., 341, #1354.
6. Diarmaid MacCulloch, *The Reformation: A History,* (New York, NY: Penguin Books, 2005), 25.
7. Ibid., 25–26.
8. Ibid., 26.
9. Rev. Reginald Garrigou-Lagrange, O.P. *Reality: A Synthesis of Thomistic Thought,* (St. Louis, MO: B. Herder Book Co., 1950), 24.
10. MacCulloch, *The Reformation: A History*, 26.
11. Libreria Editrice Vaticana, *Catechism of the Catholic Church,* 340, #1348.
12. Ibid., 342, #1357.
13. Ibid., 346, #1374.
14. Ibid., 355, #1410.

Chapter 11 Purgatory: The Great Ponzi Scheme
1. MacCulloch, *The Reformation: A History,* 12–13.
2. MacCulloch, *Christianity: The First Three Thousand Years,* 610.
3. Libreria Editrice Vaticana, *Catechism of the Catholic Church,* 345, #1371.

4. Ibid., 269, #1032.

5. Roland H. Bainton, *Here I Stand: A Life of Martin Luther,* (Nashville, TN: Abingdon-Cokesbury Press, 1950), 47–48.

6. Ibid., 69–71.

7. Eamon Duffy, *The Stripping of the Altars*, (Yale University: Worldprint, 1992) 214.

8. Nicole Winfield, "Pope urges Christmas prayers for peace," *Register-Guard*, Eugene, OR, December 26, 2015.

9. Strong, *Strong's Exhaustive Concordance of the Bible*, 28, #1722.

10. Ibid., 43, #2928.

Chapter 12 One Man's Story

1. George F. Willison, *Saints and Strangers,* (New York, NY: Reynal & Hitchcock, 1945), pg. 26.

2. Ibid., pg. 30.

3. MacCulloch, *Christianity: The First Three Thousand Years*, 748–749.